STUDY GUIDE

ENCOUNTERING A LIFE WITHOUT FEAR

STUDY GUIDE

ENCOUNTERING A LIFE WITHOUT FEAR

FULLY ACCEPTED BY OUR HEAVENLY FATHER

DR. KEVIN L. ZADAI

© Copyright 2022 Kevin L. Zadai. All rights reserved. This book is protected by the copyright laws of the United States of America. This book may not be copied or reprinted for commercial gain or profit. The use of short quotations or the copying of an occasional page for personal or group study is permitted and encouraged. Permission will be granted upon request.

Unless otherwise indicated, Scripture quotations are taken from the New King James Version. Copyright © 1982 by Thomas Nelson, Inc. Used by permission.

Scripture quotations marked (NLT) are taken from the Holy Bible, New Living Translation, copyright ©1996, 2004, 2015 by Tyndale House Foundation. Used by permission of Tyndale House Publishers, a Division of Tyndale House Ministries, Carol Stream, Illinois 60188. All rights reserved.

Scripture quotations marked (TPT) are from The Passion Translation®. Copyright © 2017, 2018 by Passion & Fire Ministries, Inc. Used by permission. All rights reserved. www.thePassionTranslation.com.

Scripture quotations marked (ESV) are from the ESV® Bible (The Holy Bible, English Standard Version®), copyright © 2001 by Crossway, a publishing ministry of Good News Publishers. Used by permission. All rights reserved.

Please note that Warrior Notes publishing style capitalizes certain pronouns in Scripture that refer to the Father, Son, and Holy Spirit, which may differ from some publishers' styles. Take note that the name "satan" and related names are not capitalized. We choose not to acknowledge him, even to the point of violating accepted grammatical rules. All emphasis within Scripture quotations is the author's own.

Cover design: Virtually Possible Designs

For more information about our school, go to www.warriornotesschool.com.
Reach us on the internet: www.Kevinzadai.com
ISBN 13 TP: 978-1-6631-0040-5

Warrior Notes Publishing
P O Box 1288
Destrehan, LA 70047

Dedication

I dedicate this book to the Lord Jesus Christ. When I died during surgery and met with Jesus on the other side, He insisted that I return to life on the earth and that I help people with their destinies. Because of Jesus' love and concern for people, the Lord has actually chosen to send a person back from death to help everyone who will receive that help so that his or her destiny and purpose is secure in Him. I want You, Lord, to know that when You come to take me to be with You someday, it is my sincere hope that people remember not me, but the revelation of Jesus Christ that You have revealed through me. I want others to know that I am merely being obedient to Your Heavenly calling and mission, which is to reveal Your plan for the fulfillment of the divine destiny for each of God's children.

Acknowledgments

In addition to sharing my story with everyone through the book *Heavenly Visitation: A Guide to the Supernatural,* God has commissioned me to write over fifty books and study guides. Most recently, the Lord gave me the commission to produce this study guide, *Encountering A Life Without Fear*, which addresses some of the revelations concerning the areas that Jesus reviewed and revealed to me through the Word of God and by the Spirit of God during several visitations. I want to thank everyone who has encouraged me, assisted me, and prayed for me during the writing of this work. Special thanks to my wonderful wife, Kathi, for her love and dedication to the Lord and me. Thank you to a great staff for the wonderful job editing this book. Special thanks as well to all my friends who know about *Encountering A Life Without Fear* and how to operate in this for the next move of God's Spirit!

Contents

Introduction..1

Chapter 1 Fear of the Lord...3

Chapter 2 Revelation Knowledge 21

Chapter 3 Every Good Path..37

Chapter 4 Sets Up Judges...51

Chapter 5 Abundant Life..61

Chapter 6 Identify Our Enemy..71

Chapter 7 Elementary Principles...81

Chapter 8 Perfected in Love..95

Chapter 9 It Will Be Done...107

Chapter 10 Extreme Assault Against the Enemy...................117

Introduction

Many people struggle with fear, and it is primarily a fear of the unknown and fear of failure. There are many unknowns, but the Holy Spirit will lead you into all truth. He will remind you of things that Jesus said and show you the future. Jesus loved you so much that He sent the Holy Spirit, and the Holy Spirit loves you so much that He is always speaking what the Father is speaking and doing what the Father is doing.

1 Corinthians 13:13 says there is faith, hope and love, but the greatest of these is *love*. That is because God is love, and perfect love drives out fear. When fear is missing, there are no limitations because your faith and hope are not contaminated. Love is ownership, and it is God declaring that you are His. You have God's name, belong to Him, and are welcome in His household. As a member of God's household, you must be raised in the fear and admonition of the Lord (Ephesians 6:4), that is, His discipline and instruction. *Freedom From Fear* is possible by getting to know God's manual; you get to know Him and then become perfected in His love!

DR. KEVIN L. ZADAI

CHAPTER 1

Fear of the Lord

These things I have spoken to you, that in Me you may have peace. In the world you will have tribulation; but be of good cheer, I have overcome the world.
—John 16:33

DISCUSSION:

Jesus said that you will have trouble in this world, but you will have peace in Him. You are to be of good cheer because Jesus has overcome the world. When you know how to deal with fear, you can live victoriously as an overcomer and have freedom from fear. You will encounter four types of fear: fear of the Lord, fear of the oppressor, fear of judgment, and fear of man.

- ❖ <u>**1 JOHN 4:18:**</u>

    There is no fear in love; but perfect love casts out fear, because fear involves torment. But he who fears has not been made perfect in love.

- Jesus said He has overcome the world, so you can too.
- You must not submit or yield to fear and to be afraid.
- You have been made perfect in the love of God.
- Perfect love drives out fear.
- You are only to have the fear of God in your life and not the fear of man, the enemy, or your future.

Fear (1828) Noah Websters Dictionary, n.

A painful emotion or passion excited by an expectation of evil, or the apprehension of impending danger. Fear expresses less apprehension than dread, and dread less than terror and fright. The force of this passion, beginning with the most moderate degree, may be thus expressed, fear, dread, terror, fright. Fear is accompanied by a desire to avoid or ward off the expected evil. Fear is an uneasiness of mind upon the thought of future evil likely to befall us. Fear is the passion of our nature that excited us to provide for our security on the approach of evil.

- Fear is something that comes suddenly upon you and is associated with either danger, harm, mischief, plague, or peril.
- Fear is in the emotional realm as a painful emotion or passion excited by an expectation of evil.
- There is also a spirit of fear, and we are not to yield to that.

FREEDOM FROM FEAR

According to 1 John 4:18, what drives out fear?

_____
_____
_____
_____

POWER, LOVE, AND A SOUND MIND

❖ 2 TIMOTHY 1:7:

For God has not given us a spirit of fear, but of power and of love and of a sound mind.

- The enemy is the one who creates fear and influences us to compromise because if we have been made perfect in love, that should have driven out fear.
- If you yield to fear, then it needs to be driven out.
- You need to address it as a spirit because Paul told Timothy that it was a *spirit* of fear.
- God has not given us the spirit of fear but of love, power, and a sound mind.

What three things allow us to overcome fear?

_____
_____
_____
_____

LIFE ABUNDANTLY

DISCUSSION:

I have been with Jesus in the Heavenly realms and encountered Him on several occasions, and I was not afraid of Jesus. When I was in the operating room, I was not afraid of dying because Jesus told me I had passed on, but I did not know I had passed on. I knew I was out of my body; looking at my body on the operating table; I could see the surgeon, his assistant, and the anesthesiologist. There is an apprehension about the unknown and about dying. We grieve for those who have passed on while we try to process the whole thing about death. Realize that it is the devil who steals, kills, and destroys. Jesus came to give us life and life more abundantly. You cannot blame God for people dying, especially if they die early, young, and tragic deaths. God allows certain things to happen, but He is not the author. He does not do terrible things to people. Often, it is because of ignorance that people are operating in the wrong thing, or they are in disobedience, especially Christians.

- ❖ **JOHN 10:10:**

    The thief does not come except to steal, and to kill, and to destroy. I have come that they may have life, and that they may have *it* more abundantly.

    - Do not be negligent but be very cautious in your walk with God.
    - The Holy Spirit wants to lead us into all truth.
    - Jesus came to give life and life more abundantly.

FREEDOM FROM FEAR

What has Jesus come to do according to John 10:10?

_____

_____

_____

_____

FACE-TO-FACE ENCOUNTERS

- **EXODUS 33:22:**
  So it shall be, while My glory passes by, that I will put you in the cleft of the rock, and will cover you with My hand while I pass by.

  - When Abraham and Moses talked to God face to face, it was not the fullness of the Father they were encountering because you could not encounter that and live.
  - The Father walked by Moses while he was in the cleft of the rock, but Moses was not allowed to see God's face.
  - The Scriptures portray an awesomeness and holiness that is beyond description, but they were not afraid of God.

- When I was outside my body, the Lord appeared to be in the room; it was the most amazing experience because I got to see Jesus in His fullness. Not in the fullness of His glory, I felt like He was allowing Himself to be approachable, but I could not look at Him.

- There is holiness and power that can come from Him, but you are not afraid of God.
- I was not allowed to look at the Father's face because of the glory coming from Him.
- Jesus appeared to many people, and they were able to talk to Him.
- Jesus sometimes holds back His glory from His Father, so we can tolerate and handle it.
- When encountering Jesus, there is awe, respect for Him, and fear of the Lord.
- If you are right with God or not, you would know it right away because of the fear of the Lord.
- Holiness creates a separateness that comes from Jesus Christ and the Godhead.

Why did God put Moses in the cleft of the rock?

_____
_____
_____
_____

HOLINESS IS OVERWHELMING

❖ 2 CHRONICLES 5:14 NLT:

The priests could not continue their service because of the cloud, for the glorious presence of the LORD filled the Temple of God.

- There are degrees that God can show you of Himself that cause you to plead for your life and repent literally.
- I felt like I was going to die, and my body could not handle it. My flesh was shaking and quaking on my bones, and the presence was so overwhelming that I repented of my sin.
- The realm I experienced was not just an awesome respect for God but so much more with no language to communicate to others.
- During revivals, this is what happens, which manifests massive repentance.
- A revelation of God's holiness and the Lord's fear is recognized.
- Solomon found himself faced down in the temple that he had built.
- The priests could not minister in their service in the temple.

What happens during revivals?

_____
_____
_____
_____

GOD ENCOUNTERS

❖ **HEBREWS 10:31:**

It is a fearful thing to fall into the hands of the living God.

❖ **<u>MATTHEW 10:28:</u>**

And do not fear those who kill the body but cannot kill the soul. But rather fear Him who is able to destroy both soul and body in hell.

- Jesus said you should not fear man, but the one who can throw your body and soul into hell.
- The Holy God we worship has such a power that emanates from Him—overwhelming, irresistible, astonishingly, and overpowering.
- I encountered this in the operating room.
- Moses, when he was on the mountain and encountering this, at times, he could handle it, and other times he could not.
- Abraham encountered God and changed his mind and changed his name.
- We should not fear man but the one who can throw your body and soul into hell.
- It is often difficult to encounter God's holiness because your flesh feels like it will die.
- During encounters with His holiness, God can change our minds and change other things about us.
- Abraham was told to leave this place and go to the place I showed him.
- Abraham made a covenant with God, and God made promises to him, which included his son, who would be born.
- God promised that everyone on earth would be related to him.

What are some things that can happen when you encounter God?

_____
_____
_____
_____

BEGINNING OF WISDOM

- **PROVERBS 9:10:**

    The fear of the LORD is the beginning of wisdom, And the knowledge of the Holy One *is* understanding.

    - Abraham's covenant was based on the fear of the Lord because of obedience, not just out of pleasure, but out of the fear of having that encounter with an awesome God.
    - Solomon said that the fear of the Lord was the beginning of wisdom, and he encountered the fear of the Lord in the temple when he dedicated it that day.

The _____ of the Lord is the beginning of _____.

GOD SPEAKS THROUGH ANGELS

❖ **GENESIS 22:12:**

And He said, "Do not lay your hand on the lad, or do anything to him; for now I know that you fear God, since you have not withheld your son, your only *son,* from Me."

- Abraham had this encounter when the angel of the Lord called to him from Heaven. He was told not to do anything with his son, for the angel knew that he feared God.
- Understand that angels will talk in the first person and will talk on behalf of God—they are prophesying.
- God is actually speaking through the angel visitation, and it is treated as if God is standing before them.
- Angel visitations can be misunderstood, and people want to bow down and worship the angels.
- Angels are fellow servants with you—you are only to worship God.
- Abraham obeyed God out of the fear of God.
- Abraham's faith is because of his obedience.
- The fear of the Lord comes with the visitation, or with the command, and revelations.
- Encounters are not occurring today because people are so busy scheduling their lives.
- We do not give time for God to be Himself and visit with us or have habitation.
- We cannot get God to move in our service by doing different things.

FREEDOM FROM FEAR

What does the fear of the Lord come with?

_____

_____

_____

_____

GOD COMES

❖ **PROVERBS 15:33:**

The fear of the LORD *is* the instruction of wisdom, And before honor *is* humility.

- You cannot produce something in a service, such as with music, and think God would be pleased with it as an offering.
- God is not impressed with some of the things we do to get Him to come and visit. Where there is no fear of the Lord, there is no holiness.
- Technology with sound systems, screens, smoke machines, and lights does not produce the fear of the Lord.
- The fear of the Lord comes because God comes.
- The fear of the Lord is the beginning of wisdom.
- The fear of the Lord brings honor, respect, and an awesome presence.
- You can be popular and have a big following, but there may be no fear of God in your life.
- When there is no fear of the Lord in a ministry, there is a disconnect from the awesome presence of the Lord.

What does the fear of the Lord bring?

_____

_____

_____

_____

DROP EVERYTHING WHEN GOD SPEAKS

❖ GENESIS 26:4:

And I will make your descendants multiply as the stars of heaven I will give to your descendants all these lands; and in your seed all the nations of the earth shall be blessed.

- Abraham was fully convinced from his encounter when God told him He would give him a son. And through that son, everyone on the earth would be blessed, and they would be as numerous as stars in the night and numerous as the sand on the seashore.
- When Abraham was initiated with all of this, he responded that he walked in the fear of the Lord.
- You must understand that Abraham dropped everything when God spoke. We see when God arrived on his property, Abraham dropped everything and ran to talk to Him.

- Our attitude should be that we fear God and give Him priority at any time and in any season.
- The angel complimented Abraham and told him that he had passed the test.
- You need to expect this also in your life because fearing God will allow you to fulfill everything God has in His heart for you.

❖ Moses was another one who feared God because he was exposed to the glory of the Father, and similarly, Jesus appeared to him.

- Many angels appeared to him because it says that the Law was actually given through angels.
- Sometimes angels will bring the fear of the Lord.
- Jesus appearing will also bring the fear of the Lord.
- The Father will manifest Himself through the glory and the glory cloud and come into services.

We should _____ everything when God speaks.

Fearing God will allow you to _____ everything God has in His _____ for you.

EMPTIED OF YOURSELF

- **EXODUS 40:34:**

  Then the cloud covered the tabernacle of meeting, and the glory of the LORD filled the tabernacle.

  - Most of the time, it takes a lot of teaching and worshipping to have the glory cloud come in a service.
  - We must be ready to receive Him, our King, the King of glory.
  - When we are not ready to receive Him, it has to do with the fear of the Lord not being manifest.

- His encounters with the Lord transformed Moses. At first, he was nervous and could not talk to anyone. But when he was in leadership in Pharaoh's court in Egypt, he became very diligent. He also killed an Egyptian to protect his people, which was a very bold and powerful thing for him to do.

  - Forty years later, God came and visited Moses and appeared to him.
  - At that time, Moses was meek and quiet and did not want to be involved.
  - His encounter with the burning bush and when his staff turned into a serpent shook Moses.
  - Moses emptied himself and was ready to be sent as the deliverer for Israel in Egypt.
  - We need to encounter the holiness of God.

- We need to encounter the Lord Himself personally at a higher level.
- We need to have the fear of the Lord operating in our lives.

❖ One way satan attacks ministers are where things become common, and they are not walking in the fear of the Lord, and they don't know it. I must always check myself, and I have been exposed to the fear of the Lord to where I thought I would die. Unfortunately, this doesn't go over well in most churches to talk this way.

- A good healthy dose of the fear of the Lord will cause you to be humble, repent, and address things like the blood of Jesus and the fear of the Lord.
- The result is that you will walk correctly and walk in the power of Jesus Christ.
- If you do not fear the Lord, you do not have wisdom.
- Moses was humble, and he was given great revelations.
- Moses managed all the miracles and the people supernaturally because of his relationship with God, where God did it.
- Moses had a huge responsibility, but he walked in humility.
- Moses encountered the Lord in a powerful way and had the fear of the Lord. The people were afraid of the awesomeness of God and observed God from a distance.
- The church does not want to go into the cloud, and everything is fine from a distance.

How was Moses able to manage all the miracles and the people?

_____

_____

_____

_____

REAL ENCOUNTER

- ❖ **<u>EXODUS 20:20-21:</u>**

    And Moses said to the people, "Do not fear for God has come to test you, and that His fear may be before you, so that you may not sin. So the people stood afar off, but Moses drew near the thick darkness where God *was*.

    - If you do not go into the cloud without real change, there is no real encounter, which means you will be ineffective.
    - When ministers back off, you can tell there is no fear of the Lord.
    - Moses could not back off because he was the only one going into the cloud and talking with God on the mountain. But every one of them was supposed to go into the cloud.
    - Moses told the people not to fear God because He had come to test them.
    - Moses wanted the people to get out of fear, the worldly fleshly fear.
    - Moses wanted the people to encounter God and to be tested.
    - The Lord's fear should be before the people.

- ❖ **There are two different fears here. You are not supposed to be afraid to die but be in perfect love, which drives out fear. When God comes in, there will be a fear, but it is a fear that causes you not to sin. Holiness is the fear of the Lord, which is interconnected to the sanctification process and is key for you to understand.**

What happens when God comes in?

_____
_____
_____
_____

PRAYER

Father, I thank You for your power, Your revelation, and that You are driving out fear. Lord, You are also revealing Yourself, and the fear of the Lord is the beginning of wisdom and causes us to be clean in the name of Jesus.

CHAPTER 2

Revelation Knowledge

...how that by revelation He made known to me the mystery
(as I have briefly written already, by which when you read, you may
understand my knowledge in the mystery of Christ),
—Ephesians 3:3-4

DISCUSSION:

The Apostle Paul had revelation from God; however, we can read Scripture and see that it is revelation knowledge—not just knowledge. If you have a degree in theology, you would not necessarily have the experience of that knowledge. You would just have knowledge. When you have only head knowledge, you can become discouraged because there is little experience and application. We want to emphasize the encounter which implements the experience. From the experience, you will have revelation and knowledge to transfer into your life. Encounters cause your relationship with God to build. Some of you have not yet had encounters with the Lord, but you will. You will encounter His holiness and the fear of the Lord. It is healthy to have the fear of the Lord in your life.

❖ Many ministers have a good message, but there is no presence. They must get back into the fear of the Lord, which means they need to encounter Him daily and not only operate in the gifts of the Spirit.

- They must also walk in the fear of God because this is how Enoch walked with the Lord (Genesis 5:24).
- When Enoch was taken up, he walked on the sapphire floor in Heaven.
- When I was in Heaven, I was allowed to walk on the sapphire floor because I walked in the fear of the Lord.
- The sapphire floor is by invitation only.
- When they get to Heaven, many people will not be able to walk on the sapphire floor because they did not walk in fear of the Lord.
- Unfortunately, this happens in every generation when we get lukewarm, and we go from one move of God to another.

What happens when you have an encounter with God?

_____
_____
_____
_____

SET THE LORD BEFORE YOU

❖ **EXODUS 20:21 NLT:**

As the people stood in the distance, Moses approached the dark cloud where God was.

- God had invited all the Israelites up there to encounter Him, but they did not want to go because they were afraid.
- You should never live afraid of the Presence of God.
- It is not God's will for a move to end because we should always be in a state of revival.
- The Spirit has already been poured out, so daily we should be living and led by the Spirit.
- Have the Lord set Himself before you, which will cause the fear of the Lord, and then you won't sin. When the fear of the Lord operates in your life, it is easy to say no to sin.
- You can say no to ungodliness and worldly passions and live an upright life in Christ Jesus.
- Invite God in with the fear of the Lord and keep the environment hot.
- Discipline is required to live in an environment hot for the Lord, but it does not happen automatically.
- You need to sow into your future for times that are coming.
- Sow into setting yourself apart, being disciplined, and concentrating on the fear of the Lord.
- Humble yourself under the mighty hand of God, and He will promote you and lift you up in due season (1 Peter 5:6).
- You cannot expect God to do something if you have not done your part first.
- When the fear of the Lord comes, there is an awe and a reverence.
- Your flesh will diminish, and your focus will be different.

❖ I remember going to the Lord and having the fear of the Lord come at the beginning of prayer because I needed to make some decisions. I gave it all to the Lord, and the power of God hit me, and I forgot why I came to pray. Those things were now gone. Whatever I was concerned about went up in a puff of smoke because of the awesome presence of God.

- You think you must pray, but you can just hand it over to the Lord and encounter God's glory.
- You encounter His fear, and it is this awesome holiness you enter.
- You forget what you were worried about and end up not praying about it because it is gone; it is done.

What happens when you have the fear of the Lord?

_____
_____
_____
_____

GO TO THE NEXT LEVEL

DISCUSSION:

The fear of the Lord will help you go to the next level, even in your prayer time where you don't find yourself begging anymore, because you change. You get onto a level with God, where you partner with Him. Jesus was in the garden and said, Listen, the enemy is coming, and you need to pray with me. They all fell asleep. He wakes them up and says, can't you even pray with me an hour so that you can endure the time of temptation that is coming upon you?

- ❖ **MATTHEW 26:40-41:**

    Then He came to the disciples and found them sleeping, and said to Peter, "What! Could you not watch with Me one hour? Watch and pray, lest you enter into temptation. The spirit indeed *is* willing, but the flesh *is* weak."

    - Jesus warned them that this was going to happen.
    - People will say that if God wants to do something, He will do it.
    - Jesus did not stop that temptation from coming.
    - Jesus warned them and told them they would enter into temptation if they did not pray.
    - They did not pass their test because the Roman soldiers came and took Jesus away.
    - None of them stayed to help Jesus or offered to go to jail with Him.
    - Jesus was warning them that they were about to sin.
    - Do not be fearful in a soulish way but yield to the fear of the Lord.

How does your prayer life change with the fear of the Lord?

_____
_____
_____
_____

YOUR PRESENCE GOES BEFORE ME

❖ **<u>EXODUS 33:15:</u>**

Then he said to Him, "If Your Presence does not go *with us,* do not bring us up from here."

- Moses and God talked to each other as a friend. Moses said, "I do not want just your presence going with me; I want your glory."
- God gave Moses his request, and this became a partnership. After a while, Moses was not fearful.
- Moses told the people that they were to go to the mountain top, but they would not go.
- The Lord said, if they did this right and loved Him and obeyed Him; He would put the fear of them and God on their enemies (Exodus 23:27).

What was the relationship between Moses and God? Give an example.

_____
_____
_____
_____

RUN TOWARD GOD

- ❖ **<u>DEUTERONOMY 28:1-2:</u>**

    Now it shall come to pass, if you diligently obey the voice of the LORD your God, to observe carefully all His commandments which I command you today that the LORD your God will set you high above all nations of the earth. And all these blessings shall come upon you and overtake you because you obey the voice of the LORD your God.

- ❖ **<u>DEUTERONOMY 28:7:</u>**

    The LORD will cause your enemies who rise against you to be defeated before your face; they shall come out against you one way and flee before you seven ways.

- ❖ **<u>EXODUS 23:27:</u>**

    "I will send My fear before you, I will cause confusion among all the people to whom you come, and will make all your enemies turn *their* backs to you.

- ❖ When I fear the Lord, I run toward God and do not run away from Him. The enemies of God and people who are not right with Him run away from that fear because it is judgment.

❖ When you partner with God, love Him, and obey Him, all these blessings will come upon you, or all these curses will come upon you if you do not respond correctly (Deuteronomy 28).

- The fear of God is going before you, and it will cause confusion among the people you come upon.
- Your enemies will leave and run in fear because they are enemies of God.
- Your enemies have become God's enemies, and God's enemies have become your enemies—it is a partnership.

What does the fear of the Lord do to your enemies?

_____
_____
_____
_____

RADIANT ONES

DISCUSSION:

The body of Christ must get to this place where it flips. What takes place is a transfer where you get your fears in order and submit to God. Then you only fear God, and not man, nor death, or fear of failure. Now you are walking with God and responding correctly, running toward Him. Suddenly, His glory is upon you, and when people encounter you, you will be radiant like Moses, reflecting God's glory and drawing others to Jesus Christ.

❖ **<u>EXODUS 34:29</u>:**

Now it was so, when Moses came down from Mount Sinai (and the two tablets of the Testimony were in Moses' hand when he came down from the mountain), that Moses did not know that the skin of his face shone while he talked with Him. So when Aaron and all the children of Israel saw Moses, behold, the skin of his face shone, and they were afraid to come near him.

- Moses had the face of God to where his face was glowing, and he had to cover it because people were afraid of him—it was because of association.
- Moses has it flipped where he was now walking with God, and that favor was on him.
- The fear of God was in Moses, and the people became afraid of Moses, just like they were afraid of God.
- All of Israel was to glow like Moses and encounter what Moses did in the cleft of the rock.
- The church is to be encountering all of this.
- We are fragmented because that is what satan and his evil spirits do here.

How do we become radiant ones?

_____
_____
_____
_____

PHYSICAL MANIFESTATIONS

- ❖ **<u>EXODUS 23:28:</u>**

  And I will send hornets before you, which shall drive out the Hivite, the Canaanite, and the Hittite from before you

    - The enemies of God had become the enemies of Israel, and they would run away. If that wasn't enough, the Lord sent hornets to drive out the enemy.
    - The people already had a spiritual fear of God which caused them to go into confusion; now, there were physical manifestations of hornets assigned and sent out to chase the people away.
    - You can expect this to happen in the present day.
    - God will work with people and try to convict them with dreams and visions at night.
    - God will use people to speak into them.
    - When they don't respond, then God must go another step.
    - God will pull away, which is not comfortable for some people.

- ❖ God will send something that will cause a physical reaction. People do not understand when this happens in other countries because it is the judgment of the Lord.

    - People cannot understand why locusts come and eat all the crops. But see, that country needs to repent. If people repented and prayed, God would hear them and send the locusts away.

- The fear of the Lord will cause people to become confused even in our leadership.
- God will do this to show as a sign that God is bringing His enemies into derision or confusion.
- The fear of the Lord will chase out the enemy.

Why does God show physical signs to His enemies?

_____
_____
_____
_____

PRAY FOR THE FEAR OF THE LORD

❖ <u>PSALM 19:9 AMPC</u>

The [reverent] fear of the Lord is clean, enduring forever; the ordinances of the Lord are true and righteous altogether.

- It is imperative that we pray for the fear of the Lord to be upon all nations and ask the Holy Spirit to bring the fear of the Lord upon us.
- In certain circumstances, people have encounters that they haven't asked for, but that is an act of grace.
- A domino effect should be initiated when the person has an encounter, talks about it, lives it, and then ministers to others.

❖ I believe the only reason all these experiences have happened to me is so that I would preach and teach the Word of God with conviction, and it will affect many people.

- Pray for the fear of the Lord.
- The fear of the Lord is the beginning of wisdom.
- God will bring knowledge, and you will be instructed and gain understanding.
- The fear of the Lord is clean, enduring forever.
- The Lord is clean has to do with sanctification and holiness.
- The judgments of the Lord are true, and they are righteous altogether.
- The fear of the Lord is part of the personality of God.
- You encounter the fear of the Lord when you get close to the Father.
- The Holy Spirit can do this for you if you ask Him.
- The Lord is holy, set apart, and there is no evil.
- Experience the fear of the Lord, encounter it, teach it, talk about these things, and you will be imparting it to others.
- You will literally be imparting a substance that has to do with the fear of the Lord.
- It is difficult to explain the fear of the Lord, but you need to encounter it and experience it for yourself.
- Wherever you go, you will shift the atmosphere, and people will sense the fear of the Lord. Then many things will happen, unwritten pages of things that will happen with the fear of the Lord—it will be almost unpredictable.

What are we to pray for?

_____

_____

_____

_____

ASK FOR TREASURE

- **PROVERBS 2:6:**

For the LORD giveth wisdom: out of his mouth *cometh* knowledge and understanding.

- What would happen if the fear of God or the glory of the Father came in? Then things will start correcting, and people's misunderstandings will be clear suddenly because a spirit of revelation is being released.

- We must receive God's words and treasure His Commands Proverbs 7:1).

- We need to incline our ears to wisdom and our heart to understanding (Proverbs 2:2).

- You need to cry out for discernment and lift up your voice for understanding (Proverbs 2:3).

- Seek and search for the hidden treasures of the Lord (Proverbs 2:4).

- You will understand the Lord's fear and find God's knowledge (Proverbs 2:5).

- The Lord stores up wisdom for the upright (Proverbs 2:7).
- The Lord is a shield to those who walk uprightly (Proverbs 2:7).
- The Lord guards the paths of justice and preserves the way of His saints (Proverbs 2:8).
- You will understand righteousness, justice, equity, and every good path (Proverbs 2:9).

❖ Many people are waiting for the Spirit of God to put this on them, and they want an encounter, but they are not asking for it.

- You have to ask for wisdom. You have to cry out for wisdom.
- You need to ask for understanding.
- You need to ask for discernment that your eyes would be sharp.
- You need to be able to divide between good and evil.
- You need to divide between your soul and your spirit.
- You need to meditate on the Word of God.
- You need to lean your ear towards what the Spirit is saying and apply it to your heart to understand.
- You need to ask God to show you where the hidden treasures of understanding are.
- You need to ask for the mysteries that have not been revealed to be revealed.
- You will seek it out, and you will find all these things.

What are we to ask God for?

_____

_____

_____

_____

PRAYER

Father, I ask that You have mercy and give us a heart that would incline to Your understanding and ears that would lean toward understanding. Father, I thank You for the impartation from Heaven of the fear of the Lord. Lord, we cry out for discernment and desire Your treasures as precious metal. Lord God, put a passion and a cry in us to ask. Holy Spirit, remind us as we cry out and walk through our day that You give us understanding. We pray that miracles, signs, and wonders begin in our life and encounter the most holy part of You, Lord. We want to walk in the holiness and sanctification and the fear of the Lord. Father, we cry out for more. In the name of Jesus, Amen.

CHAPTER 3

Every Good Path

Then you will understand righteousness and justice,
Equity and every good path.
—Proverbs 2:9

DISCUSSION:

A healthy fear causes you to be proactive for your safety and do something about it positively. However, you should not yield to fear and be paralyzed by it. When you have a bad dream, you should go to prayer right away and prevent it. You probably tapped into something the demonic is planning to do, but it does not have to happen. If you yield to that fear, you agree with it, and then something could happen. However, the fear of the Lord is the one that causes us to get into understanding.

- If we yield to the fear of the Lord and cry out for discernment, the Lord will give it to us.
- The Lord will give it out of His mouth.
- The Lord stores up wisdom.

- The Lord is a shield and a protector to those who are upright.
- The Lord guards the paths of justice and preserves the way of His saints.
- God is taking care of us; we do not need to fear.
- We will understand righteousness, justice, equity of every good path.

What does the fear of the Lord give you?

_____
_____
_____
_____

SEE AND DO GOOD

❖ **<u>PSALM 34:11:</u>**

Come, you children, listen to me; I will teach you the fear of the Lord. Who *is* the man *who* desires life, And loves *many* days, that he may see good? Keep your tongue from evil, And your lips from speaking deceit. Depart from evil and do good; Seek peace and pursue it.

- Solomon said that he is going to teach you the fear of the Lord.
- He said if you desire to have a good life and many days and see good, you must understand the fear of the Lord.
- You must learn how to pick things out and categorize them, so they become concepts, then you teach people and help them.

- The benefits of the fear of the Lord are living a long, prosperous, and good life.
- You must keep your tongue from evil and do not let your lips speak deceit.
- What ushers in the fear of the Lord is guarding your tongue and watching what you say.
- You must depart from evil and do good and seek peace.
- *Shalom* is nothing missing, nothing broken.

What are the benefits of the fear of the Lord?

_____

_____

_____

_____

PURSUE IT

❖ <u>**HEBREWS 12:14:**</u>

Pursue peace with all people, and holiness, without which no one will see the Lord:

- *Pursue* is an aggressive word because it is not like you are hoping that it comes to you. You are not sitting around waiting for it to happen.

- You pursue it because you believe that God exists and that He is a rewarder of those who diligently seek Him (Hebrews 11:6).
- However, it requires you to diligently seek Him to get rewarded.
- If you diligently seek Him, you are going to receive rewards.
- Seek peace, which is not just a peaceful atmosphere.
- Shalom means nothing missing, nothing broken, the whole covenant in operation.
- You are prospering, you are in health, your relationships are prospering, and you are driving out devils.

What does Shalom mean?

_____
_____
_____
_____

POSITIONAL AND RELATIONAL

❖ PSALM 34:15-17:

The eyes of the LORD *are* on the righteous, And His ears *are open* to their cry. The face of the LORD *is* against those who do evil, To cut off the remembrance of them from the earth. *The righteous* cry out, and the LORD hears, And delivers them out of all their troubles. *The righteous* cry out, and the LORD hears, And delivers them out of all their troubles.

- If you are classified as righteous, you have implemented the blood of Jesus into your life and are walking in obedience to the fear of the Lord. You are considered righteous, not only positionally but relationally.
- You are doing the right things, not just believing the right things.
- You are both positional and relational.
- You have applied the blood of Jesus to your life.
- You are in relationship with Him and a partaker and partner with Him in the divine nature.
- You are obeying the Holy Spirit, and that is relational.
- Now the eyes of the Lord are on you because you are righteous.
- His ears are open to your cry.
- He is not only looking at you; He is all ears to hear your cry.
- The fear of the Lord causes you to be separate, and you are not cut off.

❖ **Those who are not righteous, who are not doing good, who are doing evil, the face of the Lord is against them, and He will cut them off from the remembrance of the earth (Psalm 34:16). In other words, on earth, they will not be remembered, or they will not be mentioned.**

What does it mean to be righteous?

_____
_____
_____
_____

THE LORD IS NEAR TO YOU

❖ **PSALM 34:18 :**

The LORD *is* near to those who have a broken heart, And saves such as have a contrite spirit.

- The Lord is near if you have a broken heart right now, and you should be teaching this and encountering it.
- All those years that I was not recognized, my wife and I were doing all these things, and the Lord was teaching us and causing us to walk in the fear of the Lord.
- Many people have broken hearts, and the Lord is near to them.
- He saves those who have a contrite spirit.
- The Lord will rescue and save, and He delivers by His Word.
- For those who have a humble spirit and are willing and submissive, the Lord is all ears.
- The fear of the Lord causes humility, submission, and obedience to the Holy Spirit and the Word of God.
- A total instruction manual on encountering the fear of the Lord involves your tongue, lips, eyes, and crying out and the Lord delivering you.

The Lord is _____ to them that have broken _____ and _____ contrite spirit.

RESIST PRIDE

❖ **<u>PROVERBS 16:18:</u>**

Pride goes before destruction, And a haughty spirit before a fall.

- Ironically, being on a good path and having a broken heart is an advantage to you, even though it is not a fun process and is not God's perfect will.
- However, it produces a contrite spirit which is God's will. But unfortunately, people do not come there by themselves.
- We all know that we are stubborn. We often do not submit to the Holy Spirit, and we do not receive instruction because we have pride, and pride blinds us.
- Pride causes us to be resistant to input, so God allows us to be broken.
- When you are broken, it will produce a person who is open to hearing instruction.
- We need to cooperate with the Spirit of God.
- It is not God's perfect will for you to learn the hard way.

What does pride cause?

_____
_____
_____
_____

WHAT IS YOUR DEFAULT

- ❖ **ROMANS 8:28:**

And we know that all things work together for good to those who love God, to those who are the called according to *His* purpose.

- If being contrary to the will of God is your default system, and you constantly default to it, it was not what God wanted and was not the way it was supposed to happen.
- Lovingly, God works all things for good for those who love Him and are called according to His purpose.
- Learn these things by the Spirit instead of having to discover them by hard knocks.
- Your default system causes you not to listen and be pliable or teachable.
- Meditate on Psalm 34 and think about how God wants to help you. He loves you and is not resisting you.
- God is not keeping you from good things.
- God does not want to hurt you.
- God wants to trust you, and He needs to discipline you so that you can walk in the fear of the Lord.

What happens when you operate out of your default system?

_____

_____

_____

_____

THE DOOR TO MORE FRUIT

❖ **JOHN 15:5:**

"I am the vine, you are the branches He who abides in Me, and I in him, bears much fruit; for without Me you can do nothing."

- You are going to take the attitude that you are going to pursue these things, and God is going to give you the ability to be able to operate in these things.
- It is going to cause more manifestation, which is what God wants.
- The whole idea is to produce fruit.

❖ **MATTHEW 3:8:**

Therefore bear fruits worthy of repentance,

- The Spirit's goal is to produce fruit in your life, which should be your goal.
- You should always have the goal that you want to produce fruit in keeping with repentance.
- If you are honest with yourself, you need to say; *I want more fruit in my life.*
- It is really up to you because you are connected to the vine, and you are the branches.
- The life flow of that vine is coming through to your branch, and the fruit must come forth. It

- is impossible for God not to manifest if He is present, except when there is doubt, unbelief, and fear, and we do not submit.

❖ JOHN 14:15 AMP

"If you [really] love Me, you will keep *and* obey My commandments."

- Jesus said that if you love Him, you will obey Him, which is the door. That is the gate that opens up the life flow and causes that life flow.
- What comes through you is what produces fruit.
- Your willingness and obedience because of your love for God opens the floodgate inside you.
- Rivers of living water will rush out, and they want to manifest.
- You are going to keep with your repentance by producing fruit.
- When you stand before the Lord, you have every opportunity to open and manifest those gates inside you.

What is the Spirit's goal for your life?

_____
_____
_____
_____

FREEDOM FROM FEAR

NO FAITH WITHOUT MANIFESTATION

DISCUSSION:

There is no faith without manifestation. In between, where you have faith, you have to wait and believe. When God tells you that you will have all these different things, then to Him, it has already happened. In God's eyes, once He says something, it is done. It is impossible for God to lie, and He *will* manifest. So, fruit comes forth in your life, and it helps people around you and causes a generation to operate at a higher level so that God receives His reward for what He has done. He wants to see all He has invested through Jesus Christ by giving His Son and see the end of the age and His desires to come forth. God has faith, too, and He expects manifestation through the church and believers on earth.

- ❖ **MARK 10:27:**

    But Jesus looked at them and said, "With men it is impossible, but not with God; for with God all things are possible."

    - God is with you, and He is inside of you.
    - There is no wait or wait time anymore.
    - God breaths His Spirit on you and in you, and it will manifest, even if you are praying in the Spirit.
    - Praying in the Spirit is a manifestation from the other realm causing something physical to come out of your mouth.
    - These are words, but the Spirit anoints them.
    - Those words affect this realm as well as the Spirit realm.

With faith there is always a _____

AFFECTING TERRITORIES

❖ <u>**2 CHRONICLES 17:9-10:**</u>

So they taught in Judah, and had the Book of the Law of the LORD with them; they went throughout all the cities of Judah and taught the people. And the fear of the LORD fell on all the kingdoms of the lands that were around Judah, so that they did not make war against Jehoshaphat.

❖ <u>**2 CHRONICLES 17:12:**</u>

So Jehoshaphat became increasingly powerful, and he built fortresses and storage cities in Judah.

- The reading of the Law or the reading of the Word of God went throughout the cities.
- The fear of the Lord fell on the kingdoms, and all the lands around Judah and those people who were enemies did not make war against Jehoshaphat.
- Supernaturally, it was the pronouncement that took place from the other realm.
- The Word of God was being pronounced physically into territories, and because of that, it affected the enemies that were there to where they refused to make war.
- There was going to be war until the Law was read.
- The hearing of the Word changed their minds.

- ❖ Something spiritually happened to them because they had no reason to change their minds. They had no obligation to obey or give way to the people of God. Even today, the antichrist spirit in the world causes people not to feel an obligation to fear God or honor you for following God. Yet, when the Word of God is read and physically heard, it causes the fear of the Lord to come into the nation.

    - The media resists people reading the Word of God, preaching, and prophesying.
    - The spirit of this world is paralyzed if the Word of God is read.
    - You can stop wars literally by reading the Word of God.
    - According to Scripture, you need to speak the Word into this physical realm because it stops wars.
    - The fear of the Lord will bring peace and prosperity.

- ❖ **The fear of the Lord is strong, and you can have extreme peace, Shalom ruling. You should be using these principles in prayer, praying for our nation, your country, your state, and all things in your life, your family, and your health. Then start to teach others and build one another up in the body of Christ.**

What happens when you read the Word of God out loud?

_____

_____

_____

PRAYER

Father, in the name of Jesus, thank You for Your power. Thank You that You have anointed us to have a voice and read Your Law in all the world regions. Lord, thank You that the fear of the Lord will come upon the nations, and the people will no longer wage war against each other. But they will want to bring gifts, reward the body of Christ, and honor the body you have ordained for this time.

CHAPTER 4

Sets Up Judges

Then he set judges in the land throughout all the fortified cities of Judah, city by city, and said to the judges, "Take heed to what you are doing for you do not judge for man but for the LORD, who is with you in the judgment. Now, therefore, let the fear of the LORD be upon you; take care and do it, for there is no iniquity with the LORD our God, no partiality, nor taking of bribes."
—*2 Chronicles 19:5-7*

DISCUSSION:

We know that the Lord did not just have the Law read to the people, but He set up judges. Jesus was talking to the Pharisees and said is it not written in your Law that you are Elohim to whom the Word of God was given? And that Word can also be translated as a judge. So, you are all judges because the Word of God is given to you. Moses was given the Word of God, and he spoke it, and it was as though he was speaking for God or as God, but he wasn't God.

- **John 10:34-35 AMPC**

  Jesus answered, Is it not written in your Law, I said, You are gods? So men are called gods [by the Law], men to whom God's message came—and the Scripture cannot be set aside or cancelled or broken or annulled.

- The Word of God was given through the angels on the mountain. The Word of God says, "You are gods," or judges to whom the Word of God was given.
- They are considered gods, and Jesus said this could not be revoked or reversed. At that time, each city was set up so that judges would reinforce this Word and judge circumstances according to that Law.
- It appears as though people are gods because they are implementing the Word of God.
- Because an angel comes and speaks for God, they are not God—they speak as though they are God.
- An ambassador speaks on behalf of a person and is given special authority to represent them.
- They were not to judge for man, but for the Lord who is with you in the judgment.
- Spiritual people act on behalf of the Lord by not taking bribes, showing partiality, and not twisting or having iniquity.
- We honor everyone, and we love everyone.
- We are not doing anything unjust.

FREEDOM FROM FEAR

- ❖ When we preach the gospel, it is literally Jesus preaching His message to the people here on earth. We are sent ones, called apostles, and we represent the One who sent us.

  - We have a great commitment and responsibility to enforce and implement God's desire.
  - When we are sent ones, the judgment that we are judging is the Lord's judgment, not ours.
  - We need to be mindful that the Lord is with us, we are partakers of the divine nature, and we are partners with what God is doing.
  - We replicate what has been sent from Heaven to the earth.
  - Once we are given the Word of God, we become ambassadors.

When we are sent ones, the _____ that we are judging is the _____ judgment, not ours.

MINISTRY OF RECONCILIATION

- ❖ <u>**2 CORINTHIANS 5:18-19:**</u>

Now all things are of God, who has reconciled us to Himself through Jesus Christ, and has given us the ministry of reconciliation, that I, that God was in Christ reconciling the world to Himself, not imputing their trespasses to them, and has committed to us the Word of reconciliation.

- We have been given the ministry of reconciliation, which means we go out and pronounce to people that they have been reconciled, that the price of their sin has been paid for.
- Encourage the people to come in and accept it and have them turn themselves in, accept it, and then they are now saved.
- You must yield to the fear of the Lord and let it be upon you and not just say it, do it.
- You must allow it to have it come upon you.

What does the ministry of reconciliation mean?

_____

_____

_____

_____

CLEAN AND ENDURING

❖ <u>PSALM 19:9:</u>

The fear of the LORD *is c*lean, enduring forever; The judgments of the LORD *are* true and righteous altogether.

- You need to get understanding and allow God to implement this into your life. The fear of the Lord is clean, enduring forever.
- The judgments of the Lord are true and righteous altogether.

- The judgments of the Lord are true and righteous altogether.
- The fear of the Lord has a purity about it—it is clean and pure.
- The environment of Heaven is eternal, and it endures forever.
- Heaven has absolute truth—untarnished, unchanged, and not amendable.
- God's personality is absolute truth, and He cannot change.
- God was absolute truth as a person, and everything built is just, perfect, and valuable—an original.
- Everything came from the original and existed in the other realm that was not seen.
- You cannot change God's personality, and He will not amend Himself.
- God is not going to become impure or unclean or cease—He is going to last forever.
- God is going to influence us, and we are not going to influence Him.
- God changes not.

The _____ of the _____ is clean, _____ forever.

The _____ of the _____ are true _____ altogether.

TAUGHT WHAT IS IN HEAVEN

DISCUSSION:

The fear of the Lord comes because there is a discrepancy. Moses said to the people that they were being tested so that they would not sin and that the fear of the Lord was placed before them (Exodus 20:20). So today, on the earth, the same thing is happening. From the beginning, we never needed to be corrected. We live in a fallen world and need to rise to the occasion. In the New Testament and through teaching and understanding the fear of the Lord, we get closer to Him, even though He is inside of us.

- ❖ **PSALM 34:11-14:**

    Come, you children, listen to me; I will teach you the fear of the LORD. Who is the man *who* desires life, And loves *many* days, that he may see good? Keep your tongue from evil, And your lips from speaking deceit. Depart from evil and do good; Seek peace and pursue it.

    - Our attitude and yielding have to do with the fear of the Lord.
    - We need to have teaching on the fear of the Lord.
    - When people are not taught what is in Heaven, it does not come into the earth.
    - When wisdom speaks, you must listen—we need ears to hear.

What do we need more teaching on? Why?

_____

_____

_____

_____

STRONG CONFIDENCE

❖ **<u>JEREMIAH 17:7 NLT:</u>**

But blessed are those who trust in the LORD and have made the LORD their hope and confidence.

- Once the Spirit of the Lord has His way, it becomes a fast track and accelerates because God has your ear and heart.
- When you walk in the fear of the Lord, there is a strong confidence.
- At the end of a conference, I noticed that people left with confidence because the truth was preached session after session, and the room was saturated with worship.
- They walked into a room where there was that anointing, and the conference was saturated with the power of God in the corporate anointing; they were changed and acted differently.
- When the Spirit of the Lord enters a situation, people can do things they would normally not be able to do.
- The Book of Acts says the congregation met, prayed, and asked for boldness.

- They then spoke with boldness the Word of God even when they were told to shut up or they would be going to jail.
- They prayed for boldness and then went back out and kept preaching.

❖ **We need to get together in a corporate anointing and be built up, walk in the fear of the Lord, and have confidence. Then we can go back and operate at a different level because we encountered something in the corporate anointing. The fear of the Lord gives you strong confidence. The fear of the Lord gives you a place of refuge and safety.**

What happens when the Spirit of the Lord enters a situation?

_____
_____
_____
_____

FOUNTAIN OF LIFE

❖ **PROVERBS 14:27 NLT:**

Fear of the LORD is a life-giving fountain; it offers escape from the snares of death.

- The fear of the Lord is like a fountain, and if you picture yourself as very thirsty, you will want to drink from that fountain—it is a fountain of life. The idea is of drinking water and having eternal life.

❖ JOHN 7:38:

Anyone who believes in me may come and drink! For the Scriptures declare, 'Rivers of living water will flow from his heart.'"

- Jesus said, out of our heart, our inner man will come rivers of living water. When I was in Heaven, I saw the river of life come from the throne, flowing through us and then upward and out of us again.
- The fountain of life, which is called the fear of the Lord, comes up through us, and it drives out fear.
- Our original intent when we were created was that we would never fear or have death and sickness.
- The throne of God has that water coming forth from it, but that water is welling up in us and coming up through us, so there is no fear.
- Fear was never God's original intent.
- Fear of the Lord is the habitation, the glory that comes up from us and is perfect.
- Fear of the Lord drives out all our wrong and bad fears because it is the only correct fear we should have.
- The fear of the Lord drives out sickness and every kind of evil in us.
- The fear of the Lord drives out discrepancies.
- The glory of the Father corrects everything.
- Jesus operated in this by healing the sick, driving out devils, and raising the dead.
- You will also have that clarity to operate the same way Jesus did.

❖ **Moving forward, consider satan as a non-event and a narcissist, which means he has no conscience, is prideful, blind, and loves attention. When you do not give these evil spirits attention, ignore what they are saying, and minimalize it, they are distraught and ineffective. The fear of the Lord should be stronger in your life than the fear of what these demons are saying to you.**

Fear of the Lord is a _____ fountain; it offers _____ from the snares of death.

PRAYER

Father, in the name of Jesus, every demonic influence you may be experiencing is breaking in the name of Jesus. I command every evil spirit to leave you right now. I command every spirit of fear to leave you now. I break the devil's power over you, and the devil is a non-event in your life from now on. I silence what the evil spirits are saying to you in the name of Jesus. You are delivered by the blood of Jesus right now, and satan has been put on notice that he has been destroyed. The works of the devil have been destroyed in Jesus' name. Jesus made a show of him openly and triumphed over them, and He has brought to nothing the works of the devil. There is no power any longer that could be over you. I break that bondage in the name of Jesus and drive out fear. Father, I thank You that You are giving dreams of healing, casting out devils, raising the dead, and preaching the good news of repentance. There is the good news of debt cancellation from sin, sickness, and poverty. In the name of Jesus, I break poverty off everyone in Jesus' name, Amen.

CHAPTER 5

Abundant Life

The fear of the LORD leads to life, And he who has it will abide in satisfaction; He will not be visited with evil.
—*Proverbs 19:23*

DISCUSSION:

The fear of the Lord will lead us into abundant life, and he who has this fear of the Lord will have satisfaction, and they will abide in it, which means habitation. We all have our definition of satisfaction, whatever it takes to satisfy. But one of the benefits is we will not be visited by evil.

ABIDE IN SATISFACTION

❖ **PSALM 91:4-16:**

"Because he has set his love upon Me, therefore I will deliver him; I will set him on high, because he has known My name. He shall call upon Me, and I will answer him; I *will* be with him in trouble; I will deliver him and honor him. With long life I will satisfy him, And show him my salvation."

- Abiding in the fear of the Lord leads to long life and satisfaction.
- You will not get sick or die, but it will come upon your enemies.
- If somebody asks you where you live, you say I abide in satisfaction—it is my address.
- If you are not satisfied, you are not dwelling here.
- It is guaranteed that we will have life, a habitation called satisfaction, and a promise that we will not be visited by evil.
- We have a promise of eternal life, and life is not only in us but also around us.
- We won't have to chase evil out, and it will not visit you.
- Convince yourself to live in the fear of the Lord, abide in satisfaction, and you will not be visited by evil.
- Living this yourself, you can replicate and teach this wherever you go.
- The Word of God will be read and declared, people will hear it, and they will experience the fear of the Lord.

What does the fear of the Lord lead you into?

_____
_____
_____
_____

RICHES, HONOR, AND LIFE

❖ **<u>PROVERBS 22:4 AMPC:</u>**

The reward of humility *and* the reverent *and* worshipful fear of the Lord is riches and honor and life.

- Riches, honor, and life come by humility and the fear of the Lord.
- There are two important things needed to implement these things, mercy and grace because people are prideful.
- We are all dealing with pride, and we must adjust.
- God wants to come in and teach us how to humble ourselves under His mighty hand.
- Everyone wants riches, honor, and life, but you receive them by not being prideful and pushing yourself forward but by being humble and submissive.
- It is not a dictatorship where you project fear and control on people to get what you want—only humility and the fear of the Lord are prevalent.
- You must focus on the scripture promises that you will encounter riches, honor, and life.
- Get in the mentality of expecting these things for your life.
- You will encounter God, and He is going to change you.

What are the rewards of humility and the fear of the Lord?

_____

_____

_____

_____

HIS TREASURE

❖ <u>**ISAIAH 33:6:**</u>

Wisdom and knowledge will be the stability of your times, *And* the strength of salvation; The fear of the LORD *is* His treasure.

- When you acquire wisdom and knowledge, wisdom gives you understanding, and knowledge is being informed of the truth.
- You now have the absolute facts and truth, and then the understanding will bring stability in your times and your generation.
- It may not happen to others, but it will happen to you.
- The fear of the Lord is His treasure.
- You will have stability because of wisdom and knowledge.
- You will have the strength of your salvation or your deliverance.
- The Lord has treasure, and He distributes it to whomever He wants.
- The Lord is going to come and give you a gift.
- Anything you get from the Lord comes down from Heaven and is considered treasure, labeled as the fear of the Lord.
- The gifts inside of us influence us, and we become a treasure chest.
- Everything about this life is discovery.

FREEDOM FROM FEAR

When you have the fear of the Lord, what will you have?

_____

_____

_____

_____

COMFORT OF THE HOLY SPIRIT

- ❖ <u>**ACTS 9:31:**</u>

  Then the churches throughout all Judea, Galilee, and Samaria had peace and were edified. And walking in the fear of the Lord and the comfort of the Holy Spirit, they were multiplied.

  - There is so much inside you that it is not even known yet. God has established His kingdom inside of you.
  - He has given you all the things you need for life before birth.
  - He has already established everything we will need in Christ and given those things to us; we have already been provided for.
  - The churches throughout Judea, Galilee, and Samaria had peace and were edified, walking in the fear of the Lord and the comfort of the Holy Spirit; they multiplied.
  - The Holy Spirit comforts us.
  - The fear of the Lord was a common thing to walk in.
  - Because of the comfort of the Holy Spirit and the fear of the Lord, the church multiplied.

- Ministry needs to offer these two things, and the people experience this continually in their own life without having to be present in the church.
- When not in church, you should know God Himself and know He is there, continually and eternally.
- Press in and be diligent and experience the fear of the Lord and the comfort of the Holy Spirit.

What does the Holy Spirit bring?

_____
_____
_____
_____

CAUSE YOU TO MULTIPLY

❖ <u>**ACTS 5:14**</u>

And believers were increasingly added to the Lord, multitudes of both men and women.

- The incubator or environment conducive to growth causes the church to multiply. It equips believers to encounter this, not depending on anyone else because the Holy Spirit is all you need.
- In the Book of Acts, sometimes the church would double in the same day or a couple of days.

- There were manifestations of different profound things.
- When Ananias and Sapphira were judged in the church, it caused great fear to come upon the city and the people of God (Acts 5:1-11).
- Do not rely on others; you should be a self-feeder.

DISCUSSION:

Sheep do not wait for someone to hand them something they should eat. When you see a field where they flock together and the livestock eat, it may be bare in certain areas. So, some of the animals start to migrate to places that have not been eaten yet, and then others will follow, but it is usually certain individual sheep that lead. Yet, other animals are conditioned to know that there is a provision point for their food at a certain time and only eat there, which is predictable. However, it was up to them to eat when they were turned out. When I observed the animals in the field all day long in between that feeding point, there were open fields, and the smart sheep went to the outskirts where they hadn't been eaten yet, and they got the best. So, they were eating the best grass all day, whereas others were like it was a lot of work to find enough food where it had already been eaten.

- ❖ The Fivefold Ministry is to equip the believers to be diligent and perceptive and get the best of everything.

  - The Lord spoke to my heart and said believers are to be self-feeders.

- You should be diligent in opening your Bible and reading it, sitting there, eating it, and digesting it because you might not get anything from anyone else.
- Many times, there is a famine for the Word of God.
- The famine is about the fire, the truth from the throne, and people speaking by the Spirit and fire.
- Strong conviction is not there anymore, and it is a sign of the times.
- Dive in and seek the treasure of the fear of the Lord and the comfort of the Holy Spirit.
- You need to seek it as treasure because the Lord is giving you that treasure, but you must seek for it.

❖ When I was on the farm, it was really bad, and there was no rain, so we had to supplement feeding the animals. Mostly, they were turned out into acres and acres of land.

- I noticed some unwise that picked where it would already be picked over.
- Then there were the wise ones that went to places that were amazingly plush with grass and just ate.
- You could tell by their coat and the healthiness of their eyes, hoofs, and horns. If they were cows or horses, their coat would tell that they had been diligent and found good grass.
- God's purpose is for you not to depend upon others to feed you.
- Ask the Holy Spirit to minister to you personally.

- You will be developed as a leader and learn how to feed yourself and others.
- The Lord wants us to dig and search out His Word to develop our character.
- On earth, it is all for school and a learning process so that we qualify for eternity.

❖ Many people do not realize that if you learn it down here, you do not have to learn it in eternity. But it is not automatic, and that will be a disappointment for people. I realized when I was in Heaven that I would be learning forever. However, if I chose to be diligent and instructed, pliable, and teachable, then there was a lot of training that I did not have to go through up there. Down here on earth, you are in a learning process, and it is not like you are in the throne room all the time or in your mansion. Heaven is parallel to this realm here, but you are in a higher glory, and you will regret it when you get to Heaven if you were not diligent down here.

- Whatever you are faithful to down here, your rewards and credits carry you.
- You are going to be taught, or you are going to be teaching.
- You need to be a self-feeder and be diligent.

What do you need to become? Why?

_____

_____

_____

_____

PRAYER

I thank You, Lord, that we studied the fear of the Lord, and we understand all these things. We are going to be diligent. Father, show us where the treasure is and help us to implement it in our lives in Jesus' name.

CHAPTER 6

Identify Our Enemy

You are of God, little children, and have overcome them, because He who is in you is greater than he who is in the world.
—*1 John 4:4*

DISCUSSION:

Another fear to understand is the fear of the oppressor, and we are not ignorant of his devices (2 Corinthians 2:11); however, when the enemy comes in, we can identify our enemy and overcome them. Firmly grasp the Word of God that greater is He that is in you than He that is in the world. You need to identify these unhealthy fears in your life and deal with them. Learn how to address the fear of who is oppressing you; satan is your enemy. Evil spirits are subject to satan because they have been locked out of this realm. They are caught in the spiritual realm, slaves to satan, and they do not want to serve him, but they have no choice. The flood of Noah has disembodied them; they are trapped and not in hell but roaming the earth. Jesus stirred up evil spirits everywhere He went. The evil spirits did not want to leave the area because they had a strategic place of connection and realms of influence. Evil spirits are stationed in different places, fighting each other over territories. Evil spirits do not even like each other and are very unhappy and uncomfortable.

- ❖ You need to stir evil spirits up everywhere you go. You will be effective if you walk in the Spirit free from fear. If you fear these entities, they can manipulate your emotions and thoughts and steer you in a certain direction that you shouldn't go. Do Not be corralled by fear.

  - We cannot let these evil spirits dictate where we are going.
  - We are predictable because they place things into our thoughts and emotions.
  - Evil spirits bring people into our lives to seduce us and move us in the wrong direction.
  - You cannot fear the oppressor.
  - You cannot allow anyone who is a narcissist, who has no conscience, is cruel, mean, demanding, and critical of you to be in your life.

Why do evil spirits not want to leave an area?

_____
_____
_____
_____

FREEDOM FROM FEAR

SPIRIT OF THE AIR

❖ **EPHESIANS 2:2:**

In which you once walked according to the course of this world, according to the prince of the power of the air, the spirit who now works in the sons of disobedience.

- The prince of the power of the air that Paul talks about in the Book of Ephesians promotes fear.
- That spirit of the air, that power, is working in the world's darkness right now.
- But believers have escaped and been translated into the kingdom of light. We are not tormented any longer because torment originates with the devil.
- Fear, the spirit of fear, involves torment (1 John 4:18).
- To overcome the enemy, you must first define your enemy by defining what is God and what is not.
- You must be very well versed in the Bible and meditate on Scripture.
- Find Scriptures that define your enemy and define who God is.

What does fear involve? Describe 1 John 4:18.

_____

_____

_____

_____

STEAL, KILL AND DESTROY

❖ **<u>JOHN 10:10:</u>**

The thief does not come except to steal, and to kill, and to destroy. I have come that they may have life, and that they may have *it* more abundantly.

- In this verse, Jesus shows us the origin and the work of satan.
- If you have stealing, murdering, killing, or destroying in your life, then know that it is the enemy.
- God will never do this, and He is not working against Himself. He comes to give us life and life more abundant.
- God does not take anything from you; He is not taking life away from you, nor stealing or destroying anything—He is giving life more abundantly.
- We need to go deeper with God so that you prosper in your spirit, your soul, and your body.
- Prosperity is not just money but your health, relationships, and spiritual life.

What does the enemy come to do?

_____
_____
_____
_____

FREEDOM FROM FEAR

LOOK FOR ABUNDANT LIFE

❖ <u>**ACTS 10:38:**</u>

How God anointed Jesus of Nazareth with the Holy Spirit and with power, who went about doing good and healing all who were oppressed by the devil, for God was with Him.

- Luke wrote in the Book of Acts that Jesus was anointed by God with the Holy Spirit and power and went about doing good and healing all that the devil oppressed.
- The Father sent Jesus, so God was not working against Himself. Jesus was doing the works of the Father.
- The Father was working *through* Jesus, and He was working *with* Jesus—God was with Him.
- We, as believers, have the ministry of Jesus on the earth, and we are to do even greater works (John 14:12).
- Jesus was anointed with the Holy Spirit and with power (authority).
- Jesus went about doing good, not doing bad.
- Jesus healed the sick, not made people sick.
- God will work through you, not to tear down, but to build up, heal, drive out devils, raise the dead, heal the sick, and bring good news to the captives to break people's bondages.
- He wants you to minister from the Holy Spirit and power.
- Sickness is defined as being oppressed by the devil.
- You are to minister from the Holy Spirit and power.

What did Jesus come and do on the earth?

_____

_____

_____

_____

DESTROY THE WORKS OF THE DEVIL

- **I JOHN 3:8:**

    He who sins is of the devil, for the devil has sinned from the beginning. For this purpose, the Son of God was manifested, that He might destroy the works of the devil.

    - Jesus destroyed the works of the devil, and one of the works of the devil is clearly defined as being sickness.
    - We are going to work against sickness and not say maybe it is God's will that you were sick or that God is teaching you something.
    - You cannot teach that because that is against Scripture. Jesus was not going around and undoing what the Father was doing. He was working with the Father.
    - You cannot have any discrepancy between Jesus and the Father doing good and healing everyone.
    - You much teach correctly according to the Word of God.
    - You must teach from the Holy Spirit's power and the anointing and be fully convinced.

FREEDOM FROM FEAR

How are we to teach the Word of God?

_____

_____

_____

_____

SECRET COUNSEL

- ### **PROVERBS 3:32:**

For the perverse *person* is an abomination to the LORD, But His secret counsel *is* with the upright.

- We know that many corrupt people oppress and make people subject to them. They prosper, manipulate, control, and make it hard for others to prosper unless they are a slave to them—a narcissist mentality.
- The world powers in all the different countries and governments are driven by the enemy and oppress people.
- The perverse person is an abomination to the Lord.
- Jesus had the secret counsel of the Holy Spirit, and He did what He was told to do.
- The religious system was the only system that Jesus came against in His day.

What do the upright have from the Lord?

_____

_____

_____

_____

DO GOOD

❖ ISAIAH 1:17:

Learn to do good; Seek justice, Rebuke the oppressor; Defend the fatherless, Plead for the widow.

- The government is supposed to protect and serve the people. When they become the oppressors, we must step up to the plate and do good.
- The enemy has a plan to destroy them by pushing people and driving them.
- Jesus came to offer Himself and to offer life.
- You need to yield to the power of the Holy Spirit and do good and heal everyone.
- Do not envy the oppressor or that he is prospering.
- You are going to stay upright by listening to the secret counsel of the Lord.
- You let your relationship with God prosper, and you get counsel.
- You rebuke the oppressor and come against any evil spirit that tries to enslave.
- There are all kinds of evil spirits, smaller entities and larger ones on different levels.

- Some evil spirits rule over countries.
- The larger evil entities are diabolical.

What are we to do as ambassadors of the kingdom of God?

_____
_____
_____
_____

JESUS GAVE US AUTHORITY

❖ LUKE 10:19:

Behold, I give you the authority to trample on serpents and scorpions, and over all the power of the enemy, and nothing shall by any means hurt you.

- Jesus gave us the authority over serpents and scorpions and over all the power of the enemy, which is earthbound devils.
- All the evil spirits trapped down here from the flood, those disembodied spirits, are earthbound.
- They are stuck here until they are gathered together and thrown into the lake of fire into judgment and torment.
- The evil spirits are roaming the earth and doing the work of killing, stealing, and destroying.
- We have been given authority over the earthbound spirits.
- On earth, we have authority over devils and can break the powers and not allow them to prosper.

- Together with a corporate body, we can come against these higher levels, so they are not allowed to influence governments.
- The corporate body can unite to do intercession and warfare and take its stand in the Spirit.

What do we have authority over?

_____

_____

_____

_____

❖ Other entities have to do with other realms; we do not fully understand those things, or God would have shown them to us. Things are on other stations and places that are hard to describe, other domains that I do not fully understand. I have seen what they are in charge of and that they are princes of the power of the air. Also, there are Heavenly ones, there are earthly ones, and there are all kinds of things going on.

PRAYER

Father, I thank You for so much impartation of Heaven. We break the fear of the oppressor over us and the fear of the enemy. We are to fear no one but You. Fear is pushed out, and we drive out fear. We are made perfect through the love of God. Thank You, Father, for saturating us with Your love and driving out all fear. We love You, trust You, and obey You because we love You, in the name of Jesus.

CHAPTER 7

Elementary Principles

Therefore, leaving the discussion of the elementary principles of Christ, let us go on to perfection, not laying again the foundation of repentance from dead works and of faith toward God, of the doctrine of baptisms, of laying on of hands, of resurrection of the dead, and of eternal judgment. And this we will do if God permits.
—Hebrews 6:1-3

DISCUSSION:

The writer of Hebrews lists different subjects, and it appears that the people have already been taught these things. But do we really understand the list of things that are here? There is not a lot of teaching on this where it is definitive, but He is talking about elementary principles. We must move on to perfection and not lay the foundation again when it has already been laid. The foundation is repentance from dead works and faith in God. The subject of faith is an elementary subject, and so is repentance from dead works. Do we really understand baptism's doctrine, the laying on of hands, the resurrection of the dead, and eternal judgment?

According to Hebrews 6:1-3, what is the foundation?

_____

_____

_____

_____

TIME TO GO ON

DISCUSSION:

We must understand the fear of judgment, punishment, and eternal judgment. There will not be a Christian in hell. You will only have people who did not repent, who were thrown there because they did not believe. They did not act appropriately according to the will of God. Simply, a person must renounce Jesus to go to hell. You cannot claim to be a Christian and not live the lifestyle.

- ❖ **MATTHEW 12:31-32:**

    Therefore I say to you, every sin and blasphemy will be forgiven men, but the blasphemy *against* the Spirit will not be forgiven men. Anyone who speaks a word against the Son of Man will be forgiven him; but whoever speaks against the Holy Spirit will not be forgiven him, either in this age or in the *age to* come.

    - The only unpardonable sin mentioned in the Bible, the one that is not forgivable, is when you are a Christian and stand up publicly and say that you do not want to be a Christian anymore. You do not believe in Jesus Christ and want to reject Him publicly.

- There is no repentance, no turning back from that sin—only fearful judgment after that.
- Rejecting Christ is the only way a so-called Christian can go to hell, according to the Bible.
- Eternal judgment is something that is forever, and God is the only one able to do that kind of judgment.
- We do not have the power to send somebody to hell.
- People go to hell because they decided to go there—it is between God and them.
- Christians should never fear eternal judgment—it is forbidden.
- Christians in Heaven will be judged according to what they did with what they were given.

❖ JOHN 14:6:

Jesus said to him, "I am the way, the truth, and the life. No one comes to the Father except through Me.

- Jesus is the way, the truth, and the life, and you have to accept Him.
- You love the Lord, and you obey Him.
- The people in Heaven who did not do exactly what Jesus had written about them still make it to Heaven, but there are no rewards for disobedience.

❖ 1 CORINTHIANS 3:13-15:

Each one's work will become clear; for the Day will declare it, because it will be revealed by fire; and the fire will test each one's work, of what sort it is. If anyone's work which he has built on *it* endures, he will receive a reward. If anyone's work is burned, he will suffer loss; but he himself will be saved, yet so as through fire.

- Paul says if anyone's work is burned, he will suffer loss, but they will be saved as through the fire, but they barely make it through.
- Your spirit is made new, and old has passed away (2 Corinthians 5:17).
- Heaven is your home, and there is no fear of judgment or fear of punishment there.
- You do not speed on the highway because you fear getting caught, but you obey the law.
- Christians should not need the law. We should be able to do it from our hearts because we love God and people. So, we don't sin, and we don't break the law.
- You do not have a fear of punishment because you did not do anything wrong.

Explain 1 Corinthians 3:13-15.

_____

_____

_____

_____

FREEDOM FROM FEAR

❖ You do not fear getting in trouble with God every day if you do something wrong. You think about how much you love God and how your heart is right. You ask the Lord for help, but you do not have a fear of punishment or judgment. You walk in the fear of the Lord because you love God and obey Him.

- We need to get past the fear of judgment and the fear of punishment and graduate.
- When you are always repenting, you do not think about getting into trouble with the Lord.
- Always keep it clear and right before the Lord.
- You need to have a fear of the Lord, but not a fear of punishment.
- Always be in repentance; it is not just a one-time occurrence.
- You will not be thrown into eternal judgment because you were off course.

Christians are not to have a fear of _____ or the fear of _____.

MAKE A COURSE CORRECTION

DISCUSSION:

Even though you might be off course at times in your life, it will take a minor correction to get back on course. It is not like you will be thrown into eternal judgment because you are off course. You must come back to the Lord. He is a loving Heavenly Father who will make it right and help you. So come to Him because you will not be afraid of punishment. I turn myself in and ask for mercy. I ask for God's help. You should be able to run to your Heavenly Father no matter what. Don't fear eternal punishment, and don't fear judgment.

❖ 1 THESSALONIANS 5:9:

For God did not appoint us to wrath, but to obtain salvation through our Lord Jesus Christ,

- Make course corrections based on the Holy Spirit helping you every day.
- You are a child of God, and you have been adopted.
- We have come to the knowledge of the truth, and we no longer willfully sin because we don't need to.
- We have eternal life, and the Spirit helps us in our weakness.
- Continually allow the Holy Spirit to give you course corrections and keep you in line.
- If you become an adversary of God, which is working against Him, there is a fearful expectation of judgment and indignation.
- If you have the Spirit of God in you, why would you want to work against God in any way?
- It is up to you to decide which side of the fence you will be on.
- Christians should not be afraid of punishment.

❖ **HEBREWS 12:5b-7:**

"My son, do not despise the chastening of the LORD, Nor be discouraged when you are rebuked by Him; For whom the LORD loves He chastens, And scourges every son whom He receives." If you endure chastening, God deals with you as with sons; for what son is there whom a father does not chasten?

- God disciplines those He loves, but discipline is not punishment but a course correction. God does not want you to get hurt, so He might discipline you to get you to stay away from things that hurt you. But you should be able to decide for yourself and just not do it.
- Sometimes you need discipline because He must teach you and mentor you, but it is not punishing you.
- God might cause restrictions in your life, and you should not be afraid of Him.
- You should only be afraid as a Christian when you decide to work against God and do not want to be a Christian anymore; then, there is a fearful expectation of judgment.
- The Lord says that vengeance is mine, I will repay (Romans 12:19).
- The Lord will judge His people, and you must separate yourself from anyone working against the Holy Spirit.

Why shouldn't you despise the chastening of the Lord?

_____
_____
_____
_____

THE LINE IS DRAWN

DISCUSSION:

When you speak against the Holy Spirit, that is not forgivable. "Therefore I say to you, every sin and blasphemy will be forgiven men, but the blasphemy *against* the Spirit will not be forgiven men" (Matthew 12:31). If you work against the Holy Spirit, Jesus said in other words, "You can say bad things about My Father, you can say bad things about Me, but if you speak against the Holy Spirit, you will not be forgiven in this life or the next." You must remember that this is where the line is drawn, and these things cannot be revoked. Understand that some people feel they have gone to that line, but they have remorse—that is how they know they have not done it. Your conscience would be seared if you committed the unpardonable sin. If you have remorse and you repent, that is different. If you continue to speak against the Spirit of God and the ministry of the Holy Spirit, you are on shaky ground. You should have a fearful expectation of judgment. Scriptures say, "Vengeance is mine; I will repay," says the Lord (Romans 12:19). Stay clear of people who speak against the Holy Spirit because they work against God. I have known people in my Bible class who told me they did not want Jesus anymore. They said they knew what they were doing and did not care. When I tried to pray for that person, I was not allowed to pray for them. Unfortunately, this is serious business. Sadly, that person will spend eternity in hell.

- ❖ The Apostle Paul was ignorant and did not know what he was doing when he attacked Christians. He thought he was doing God a favor by killing the Christians until Jesus visited him. He then realized he was working against the people of God and God's purpose (Acts 26:12-18).

FREEDOM FROM FEAR

- ❖ Our enemy, satan, uses all these kinds of things to twist Scripture and get Christians to think they have committed the unpardonable sin.

  - Then satan causes them to have this fear of punishment and eternal judgment, but it is not true.
  - We need to help everyone and get the body of Christ out of sin consciousness and out of condemnation and the fear of being punished and having eternal punishment and judgment.
  - However, if you meet someone whose conscience is seared, and they could care less, it is not worth your time because the person obviously has already committed the unpardonable sin, and there is no repentance for them.

What is the unpardonable sin?

_____
_____
_____
_____

WELL PLEASING TO HIM

- ❖ **<u>2 CORINTHIANS 5:9-11</u>**

  Therefore we make it our aim, whether present or absent, to be well pleasing to Him. For we must all appear before the judgment seat of Christ, that each one may receive the things *done* in the body according to what he has done, whether good or bad. Knowing the terror of the Lord, we persuade men; but we are well known to God, and I also trust are well known in your consciences.

- We make it our aim to be well pleasing to Him and are well known to God, but we are well known in our conscience also.
- You should not be thinking about judgment and punishment but about pleasing God.
- We should be teaching others how to please God because He is the one we are concerned about.
- We all must appear before the judgment seat of Christ, not the judgment seat of the world.
- The people of the world are judged in a different judgment, but we are judged at the seat of Christ.
- I already had this happen to me, I had my audit, and then I was sent back to earth.
- The judgment seat of Christ is based on what you did with what you were given.
- The world is judged on what they knew and what they did with what they knew.
- If the person does not accept Christ, then the Lord decides that they are going to hell.
- We, as Christians, will receive rewards for the things we have done in the body.
- There are no rewards for the bad things Christians have done.

❖ Christians receive a report card where they have invested whatever talents they had and what they did with them.

- How many souls were saved, and people changed and helped?
- Angels record all the acts of kindness you do.
- You receive rewards eternally, and it goes into your account.
- All your rewards in Heaven are based on what you did in the flesh.
- There will be many treasures and rewards in Heaven for people doing amazing things.

Why do we receive rewards in Heaven?

_____
_____
_____
_____

INVESTING IN THE KINGDOM

❖ **<u>COLOSSIANS 3:23:</u>**

And whatever you do, do your work heartily, as for the Lord and not for people.

- While you are in the flesh, use every gift working extra to help the poor and give to people. Believe God for prosperity so that you can continue to increase your giving, and God will supernaturally provide finances.

- We are supposed to be investing in the kingdom. We are ambassadors, and we have a ministry of reconciliation.
- Go out and persuade men or compel them to come into the kingdom.
- As ambassadors doing the work of the ministry, we are known by God.
- There is no judgment or punishment for Christians.
- You will be rewarded for how you invested your talents and the return on that. You give back what was given to you.
- If you sing, how often did you sing? Did you sing songs to the Lord?
- The same is true with writing, teaching, art, or anything you did.
- Did you do something to glorify your Father God and help people?
- There are no rewards if you do not do anything for Christians.
- The judgment seat is more of an audit of what you did with what you were given.
- Things will be taken away if you do not do what you are supposed to, but you still make it to Heaven.
- The wood, hay, and stubble will be revealed by fire.
- Only the gold and silver and precious things will survive this audit.

❖ **You must make a decision that you are going to serve the Lord, and you are not going to deny Him. You are going to walk with Him. What you get from the reward system is based on how you discern your gifts and talents. If you can cook or grow a garden, are you giving a portion to someone else? You have a healthy fear of the Lord, which means you will not do certain things and will not judge yourself wrongly. The fear of the Lord is healthy, clean, and causes you to be separate.**

What are you supposed to do with your gifts and talents?

_____
_____
_____
_____

PRAYER

Father, I thank You that no one will have condemnation about judgment and fearfulness that they have committed the unpardonable sin. I break the lie of the devil over them. I thank You, Lord, for restoring their life and taking them into Your fullness. There is no fear of judgment because there is repentance. I thank You, Father, that You love us and do not want anyone to go to hell. Thank You, Lord, that You purchased us and that we are not afraid of eternal judgment. Thank You, Lord, that You have a home for us, and we will be with You forever. Thank You, Father, that we will work in the fear of the Lord and do the work of the ministry, and we will see rewards for that in Jesus' Name. Amen.

CHAPTER 8

Perfected in Love

Love has been perfected among us in this: that we may have boldness in the day of judgment; because as He is so, who are we in this world. There is no fear in love; but perfect love casts out fear, because fear involves torment. But he who fears has not been made perfect in love. We love Him because He first loved us.
—1 John 4:17-19

DISCUSSION:

There is no fear in love, but perfect love casts out fear, and fear involves torment. But he who fears has not been made perfect in love. We love Him because He first loved us. The goodness of God draws us and causes us to repent (Romans 2:4). Christians have a sin consciousness when they should have a righteous consciousness. There should be no fear in your life because God is love, and He is perfecting us. Love has been perfected in us, and we have boldness on the day of judgment. You will not be judged if you are bold and sure of yourself. You will be before Him and see Him as He is; we are like Him in this world (1 John 3:2). We are already separate, and we are different. Do not waste your time trying to fit in down here. Do not feel guilty for past sins if they have been forgiven.

- ❖ If you have sin consciousness, you will make mistakes because you are unsure. When you are perfected, you will know it because you will have boldness.

    - You have a position in Christ but also a relationship with the Lord.
    - You have been made perfect in love.
    - Love casts out or drives out fear. It is literally taking a whip and driving out the devils, driving out fear and casting it out.
    - Fear has to do with torment and demons.
    - When you feel fear, immediately let God saturate you with His love and drive out fear.
    - You need to be restored to this place, so you are bold.
    - If a person is not bold, they are not established and well informed about fear.
    - Fear drives us to do sinful things.

- ❖ When I talk to people and ask, "Why did you do that? What happened?" They will often say that they were fearful or felt rejected. Evil spirits are making them feel like a victim, and they are not. Because of that, they committed things that they would not have done.

    - Those demons are hijacking you and your life. You have got to stop it

- We love Him because He first loved us (1 John 4:19).
- He chose to do everything He was doing for us before we were born.
- Fear is finished because we are done with torment.
- God has forgiven you, so there is no fear of punishment or fear of torment.
- There is no judgment because you are to judge yourself lest you be judged (1 Corinthians 11:31).

What does perfect love produce?

_____

_____

_____

_____

TURN YOURSELF IN

❖ **<u>ZECHARIAH 1:3:</u>**

Therefore say to them, 'Thus says the LORD of hosts: "Return to Me," says the LORD of hosts, "and I will return to you," says the LORD of hosts.

- Daily you need to repent and keep yourself continually with a clear record.

- Jesus Christ comes in by His Spirit and allows you to operate in this power, so do not hesitate. You have been made perfect in love.
- People who operate in evil spirits are motivated and propelled by an evil spirit and create a fear of man. They create a scenario where you are afraid of what people think.
- All fear and tormenting spirits are driven out, and its power is broken.
- All lying spirits coming against you are destroyed.

What are you to daily keep yourself in?

_____
_____
_____
_____

TRUST IN THE LORD

❖ <u>PROVERBS 29:25:</u>

The fear of man brings a snare. But one who trusts in the LORD will be protected.

- If you trust in man and fear man, you become enslaved to a man, a snare. But if you trust in the Lord, you will be safe.
- You must decide to have faith in God to take care of things, or will you be subservient to a person and enslaved in your mind to try to please people? You will never please people.

- The evil spirits will ensure that you are ensnared to a person, and that person will never be completely satisfied because that is how a narcissist works. Evil spirits work this way, and satan is a narcissist.
- Evil spirits use and manipulate people through fear.
- When you fear that person, that is a snare, and it is hard to get out of it.
- Trust in the Lord, and do not let fear dominate you, especially when it has to do with men—it is in the flesh.
- Evil spirits manifest through people.
- We are to have a healthy fear and respect for those in authority, and they are supposed to protect us.
- Sometimes there is an evil matrix you must pray through because people can be entrenched in evil controlling spirits and be your relative, co-worker, boss, etc.

What does the fear of man bring?

_____
_____
_____
_____

DO GOOD

❖ <u>**ROMANS 13:1-4:**</u>

Let every soul be subject to the governing authorities. For there is no authority except from God, and the authorities that exist are appointed by God. Therefore whoever resists the authority resist the ordinance of God, and those who resist will bring judgment on themselves. For rulers are not a terror to good works, but to evil. Do you want to be unafraid of authority? Do what is good, and you will have praise from the same. For he is God's minister to you for good. But if you do evil, be afraid; for he does not bear the sword in vain; for he is God's minister, an avenger to *execute* wrath on him who practices evil.

- You need to develop your character where you become bold and operate in your God-given authority.
- If you are doing everything correctly, it should not be a terror to you. His presence should be a comfort, not a curse.
- We can live without fear when we do what is right.
- When we do what is wrong, we fear being caught.
- You are afraid of being caught instead of having the fear of the Lord and then just not doing it.
- There are consequences for what you are doing, and if you are doing wrong, it is a matter of time before you get caught.
- You should do or not do things out of the fear of the Lord, not of what I can get away from.

How are we to live?

_____
_____
_____
_____

FREEDOM FROM FEAR

CULTIVATE AND GROW IN LOVE

- ❖ **<u>COLOSSIANS 1:10:</u>**

    …that you may walk worthy of the Lord, fully pleasing *Him,* being fruitful in every good work and increasing in the knowledge of God;

    - You need to cultivate your spiritual life, grow in love, honor Him, and not neglect the things that cause you to prosper. That is your prayer life and understanding of the Word of God.
    - The Father wants to use you and to get a return on what He has invested in you.
    - Do not think about getting caught, do not speed, and do not cheat.
    - Make decisions every day to do good things.
    - We are to cultivate and do righteousness and grow in love, which causes us to do everything correctly so that we do not fear getting caught.

How are we to walk with the Lord?

_____
_____
_____
_____

LEARNED OBEDIENCE

❖ **<u>HEBREWS 5:7-9</u>:**

…who, in the days of His flesh, when He had offered up prayers and supplications, with vehement cries and tears to Him who was able to save Him from death, and was heard because of His godly fear, though He was a Son, *yet* He learned obedience by the things which He suffered. And having been perfected, He became the author of eternal salvation to all who obey Him.

- Jesus was a child who grew up, learned, and was nurtured by the Word of God, growing in the fear of the Lord.
- He matured to where He called His mother *woman* one day.
- Jesus switched over and became the Man who the Spirit-anointed, the Messiah, who was God in the flesh.
- There came a place where He did not define those who followed Him. Jesus pointed to the crowds He was teaching and called them His family.
- Then He had to suffer and go to Jerusalem and die.
- Jesus had to do the Father's work now.
- Jesus was motivated by Godly fear and cried out to God for help in the flesh.
- Even though He was the Son of God, He learned obedience by the things He suffered.
- He had to do what His Father wanted Him to do versus what His family wanted Him to do.

❖ We, too, must have the rubber meet the road and say, "I am going to please God and not man."

- Jesus was disciplined, and He learned that discipline from what He suffered.
- He had to obey God, which means He had to leave His family.
- He separated Himself, and He suffered for it because He was not going to succumb to the fear of man.
- Jesus obeyed the Father so that all who obeyed Him would have eternal life.
- Jesus wants us to tend to our spiritual life by cultivating and growing in the knowledge of God.
- Jesus was perfected in love, separated Himself, and was not operating in the fear of man.

How do we learn obedience?
_____
_____
_____
_____

FAITH MEANS TRUST

❖ **<u>HEBREWS 6:18 NLT:</u>**
So God had given both his promise and his oath. These two things are unchangeable because it is impossible for God to lie. Therefore, we who have

fled to him for refuge can have great confidence as we hold to the hope that lies before us.

- When talking about faith, it is interesting that faith means you trust. The opposite of trust is not trusting.
- Why don't you trust someone? There may be a good reason you don't trust someone, but you should trust God.
- If you have a fear of the unknown or a fear of failure, these things will keep you from trusting God.
- In the Old Testament, the word for faith is really the word trust. And trust had to do with a track record, relationship, and covenant.
- It simply comes down to a person keeping their word.
- If a person keeps their word, you have faith in that person.
- If God keeps His Word to you, then you can trust Him.
- Faith is literally saying that if God said something, He had the title deed and gave you the title deed, which is the evidence of what you cannot see (Hebrews 11:1).
- Faith is the evidence of things in the spirit ready for you that God proclaims to you before you receive them.
- Trust is faith.
- Faith is the complete transaction, but it might not manifest immediately.
- Abraham was 100 years old but trusted God that Sarah would have a son. Abraham was perfected in love to where he trusted God.
- Trust is interpreted as fearing God. The fear of the Lord, trusting God, and having faith in God are all congruent.

- If God says something, it does not matter what happens in the flesh or the physical because God's Word is who He is as a person.
- God will give you the title deed, and the evidence is faith.

It is impossible for God to _____.

MORE VALUABLE

❖ <u>**MATTHEW 6:28-30:**</u>

So why do you worry about clothing? Consider the lilies of the field, how they grow: they neither toil nor spin; and yet I say to you that even Solomon in all his glory was not arrayed like one of these. Now if God so clothes the grass of the field, which today is, and tomorrow is thrown into the oven, *will* He not much more *clothe* you, O you of little faith?

- Jesus is teaching us not to worry because worry has to do with fear.
- Worry will not benefit you in any way.

Why are we not to worry?

_____
_____
_____
_____

CHAPTER 9

It Will Be Done

Then Jesus said to the centurion, "Go your way; and as you have believed, so let it be done for you." And his servant was healed that same hour.
—Matthew 8:13

DISCUSSION:

You can develop a relationship with God where you know He will not fail you, which can be a big step for most Christians. We are called to make that big step into smaller and easier steps. You will learn by baby steps through trust and relationship with God, knowing that you can depend on Him. He depends upon you, and you depend upon Him. It is a relationship, as a covenant, and there is no fear. You should be spending your energy doing something about it, like prayer, and then going and doing what you can do. Sometimes you have to do things because you need to do them. You need to be productive and trust God along the way, and He will make it work out. God will prosper you when you do not have a lack of faith.

❖ **MATTHEW 8:10:**

When Jesus heard *it,* He marveled, and said to those who followed, "Assuredly, I say to you, I have not found such great faith, not even in Israel!

- This man was a Roman soldier, who did not have a covenant with God, and yet Jesus granted his request because he believed that by speaking the Word, it would be done.
- Jesus said that there would be many who do not have this kind of faith.
- Unfortunately, the people of Israel did not discern the day of visitation, and Jesus said that he was sent to the lost sheep of Israel.

What did Jesus marvel at?

_____

_____

_____

_____

SPEAK THE WORD

❖ **MATTHEW 8:26-27:**

But He said to them, "Why are you fearful, O you of little faith?" Then He arose and rebuked the winds and the sea, and there was a great calm. So the men marveled, saying, "Who can this be, that even the winds and the sea obey Him?"

- If you are fearful, you have little faith.
- You cannot have fear and have faith and trust working at the same time.
- The men marveled that the winds and the waves obeyed Jesus and became calm. The disciples did not discern who Jesus was and were not trusting His Word.
- Our relationship has much to do with our faith. When God gives you His Word, that is the title deed, the evidence that you received what you have not seen.
- Realize that according to your faith, it will be done to you, and you can displace all fear, doubt, torment, and worry because of your relationship with Jesus.
- You are perfected in love and perfected in faith
- You discern God and trust His Word.

When God gives you a Word, what does it become?

_____
_____
_____
_____

PERFECT FAITH

❖ **<u>HEBREWS 11:1-6:</u>**

Now faith is the substance of things hoped for, the evidence of things not seen. For by it the elders obtained a *good* testimony. By faith we understand that the worlds were framed by the word of God, so that the things which are seen were not made of things which are visible. By faith Abel offered to God a more excellent sacrifice than Cain, through which he obtained witness that he was righteous, God testifying of his gifts; and through it he being dead still speaks. By faith Enoch was taken away so that he did not see death, "and was not found, because God had taken him:: for before he was taken he had this testimony, that he pleased God. But without faith *it is* impossible to please *Him*, for he who comes to God must believe that He is, and *that* He is a rewarder of those who diligently seek Him.

A REWARD SYSTEM

❖ **<u>HEBREWS 11:6:</u>**

But without faith *it is* impossible to please *Him,* for he who comes to God must believe that He is, and *that* He is a rewarder of those who diligently seek Him.

- The kingdom has a reward system for everything you do, which is the substance of things hoped for.
- Jesus has granted you the title deed, and you might not be able to see it, but it is a legal document and belongs to you.
- Knowing that God is not going to deceive you is faith and trust.
- You are free from fear because God spoke to you, and you will have it.
- You should hear from God and know there is a way out of everything you are going through.

For he who comes to God must _____ that He is a _____ of those who diligently seek Him.

FREEDOM FROM FEAR

- ❖ You will be free of fear when you are in perfect love and faith. When we mentioned things hoped for, this is where the word title deed comes in for things not seen.

  - The generals of faith obtained a good testimony because they understood that a substance was given to them from the other realm inside them.
  - They decided not to doubt and fear and understood God. When God said He would do it, that was it, period.
  - God took something from the other realm, spoke it, and it came into this realm.
  - Everything that was made was made through Jesus Christ.
  - If He spoke you into existence and wrote a book about you, He can make anything He wants to come to pass in your life.
  - God can make something out of nothing.
  - Enoch was taken because he pleased God.
  - Without faith, it is impossible to please Him.
  - Faith is trust, relationship, and covenant.
  - There is a confidence that you know that God exists, and He rewards those who diligently seek Him.
  - Jesus could minister to people because they discerned who He was and knew God's Word was true.
  - The people trusted in the Prophets, they trusted in the Word of God, and they trusted in Jesus because He fulfilled prophesy.

What is faith?

_____
_____
_____
_____

AGGRESSIVE FAITH

- ❖ **<u>MARK 11:22-24:</u>**

    So Jesus answered and said to them, "Have faith in God. For assuredly, I say to you, whoever says to this mountain, 'Be removed and be cast into the sea' and does not doubt in his heart, but believes that those things he says will be done, he will have whatever he says. Therefore I say to you, whatever things you ask when you pray, believe that you receive *them*, and you will have *them*.

- When you trust in Him, who He is, and His Word, you do not have doubt, fear, and worry, but you now operate in an aggressive faith.
- In other words, you do not wait until you get what you prayed for, you believe, you steadfastly hold the title deed, and God will do what He said He would do.
- So, when you ask, you receive by being in the realm of believing, trusting, and knowing that God is going to do it.
- Rest assured, He is not only able and willing, but He wants to do it, He desires to do it, and He will do it—perfect love and faith.

- Whoever prays with this kind of faith always receives because it is the assurance of things hoped for.
- You have the evidence of things not seen.
- When you pray, you already believe that you have received them already.
- You see the title deed in your hand.
- You see the evidence as you are praying, not after you prayed, and not when it comes.
- You see it as you pray, and as you are praying, you do not have any unforgiveness.
- Forgive everyone and let it drop because this will hinder you.
- You will be able to receive, and Jesus puts no limitations on us.
- Jesus never said there are certain things we cannot ask to be removed or ask for.
- What you say with your mouth, you believe in your heart that what you say will be done.
- Jesus wants us to trust Him, but for us to be actively, aggressively, asking, believing that we will receive—on the offensive, not defensive.

When you pray, what should you believe? What can hinder your prayer?

_____

_____

_____

_____

❖ I wait until God tells me about my mountains or anything that is in the way. I let Him dictate these things that are in the way, then I speak to Him, knowing that God has already labeled it as something in the way.

- God gives me the authority to speak it, but I believe I receive it as I pray.
- God has defined it as a mountain, and it must be removed.
- God is not going to remove things for us.
- He tells us to speak to the mountains and remove them; we must believe by faith.
- We have authority down here, and through the church, God will use us to move things out of the way.

❖ **If something bad happens in our country, it is up to us to stop these things and to be aggressive. It shows the lack of faith and unity on earth when we do not get together, pray, and move mountains. We are dealing with things because we have let them happen. We need to return to the body of Christ and the church where the gates of hell cannot prevail against that church (Matthew 16:17-19).**

What does it show when we do not get together and pray to move mountains?
_____
_____
_____
_____

- ❖ You are adopted if you discern Jesus as the Savior, the Messiah, and the Deliverer. You have eternal life and these other benefits as well. We are to glorify God here on the earth.

  - Jesus said you could ask whatever you desire, and it will be given to you so that My Father will get the glory to Himself (John 14:13).
  - And Jesus said, ask that your joy would be made full (John 16:24).
  - We now have the title deed.
  - We have the blood of Jesus. We have been adopted in.
  - We have a greater covenant with better promises.
  - Do not allow anything that has happened in your life to hurt you.
  - Forgive everyone.

What is aggressive faith?

_____
_____
_____
_____

PRAYER

Father, I thank You that we are not going to worry anymore. We trust You. We thank You for the blood of Jesus, and we are not offended. We forgive everyone. We will not worry, doubt, or fear, and we break fear in the name of Jesus. We are going to prosper in everything we put our hands to doing. Father, because we are doing Your perfect will on this earth. We thank You that You have handed us the title deed for the answers to our prayers, and we pray in the name of Jesus.

CHAPTER 10

Extreme Assault Against the Enemy

The LORD your God in your midst, The Mighty One, will save;
He will rejoice over you with gladness, He will quiet you
with His love, He will rejoice over you with singing.
—*Zephaniah 3:17*

DISCUSSION:

The Lord gave me an amazing vision and a powerful revelation of Him as a warrior. There is an aggressive side of the Lord where He is not just sitting on a throne, being served, and worshiped. He is also very aggressive toward His people and helps them with His purpose and plans. Now we will talk about warfare, an extreme assault against the enemy, and how we can come against fear. When they are in a war, most people hunker down and wait for it to stop. Sometimes it is not going to stop unless you do something about it. And this is where your faith destroys fear by being aggressive in who you are in Christ and your authority. We are to minister in the power of the Spirit and the gifts of the Spirit. Christ anoints you to do the same works that He did.

- We need to frame our minds correctly in who we are in Christ.
- We have the power to change history and the direction of generations to come.
- The Lord Jesus Christ is rising the church up in maturity, and the Bride is being made ready for the marriage.
- We have received impartations from Heaven, but it is time to wage war because the Lord is a warrior.

❖ **The Lord is a warrior, and He is in the midst of you. He is righteous and Holy and drives out evil spirits. If the Lord shows up, evil spirits will flee, which means that fear will flee from your life. If He is in your camp, house, job, and church, He will drive out fear and break some yokes.**

THERE IS A CLEANUP

❖ <u>**GALATIANS 5:1:**</u>

Stand fast therefore in the liberty by which Christ has made us free, and do not be entangled again with a yoke of bondage.

- I want to educate people to drive out devils, so they never return.
- You can have all the yokes taken off you, devils can leave, but there could be bondage, and things need to be taken care of—healed and removed.
- God will break those yokes that the devils have established in people.
- It is an aggressive thing, but it is not just Him showing up; it is the fact that there is a cleanup.

FREEDOM FROM FEAR

- Healing has taken place, and there is deliverance that goes on.
- He is in your midst. He is rejoicing over you.

JOYFUL SONGS OF DELIVERANCE

❖ ZEPHANIAH 3:17 NLT:

For the LORD your God is living among you. He is a mighty savior. He will take delight in you with gladness. With his love, he will calm all your fears. He will rejoice over you with joyful songs.

- The Lord sings songs of deliverance over you.
- He is a mighty savior.
- He is in your mess, and He is rejoicing over you.
- He is not mad and not criticizing you.
- He will take delight in you with gladness.
- His love will calm all your fears.
- He is happy and rejoicing over you, singing joyful songs about your deliverance.

How does God calm all your fears? How does He rejoice over you?

_____
_____
_____
_____

THE BATTLE IS THE LORD'S

DISCUSSION:

I believe His voice breaks yokes over you and the battles you are going through are the Lord's battles because He is in your midst. The devil fights this aggressiveness of the gospel when you know that you are no longer a victim. The devil does not want Christians to mature and become aggressive in their faith. You need to start talking about the Holy Spirit, ministering in the power and gifts of the Spirit, and speaking in tongues. Even the church and religious people will come against it when you start talking about these things.

❖ **<u>1 SAMUEL 17:47:</u>**

Then all this assembly shall know that the LORD does not save with sword and spear; for the battle *is* the LORD's, and he will give you into our hands.

- The Lord is driving out devils.
- The Lord is driving out poverty, debt, and sickness.
- The Lord is driving out any kind of dysfunction in your life.
- The Lord is breaking yokes.
- The Lord is breaking failure in your life.
- The Lord turns things around, and there is deliverance.
- The Lord is speaking Good News to you and singing songs of deliverance over you.
- The Lord will win because He knows it is His battle.

FREEDOM FROM FEAR

WEAPONS OF WAR

- ❖ <u>**1 TIMOTHY 1:18-19:**</u>

This charge I commit to you, son Timothy, according to the prophecies previously made concerning you, that by them you may wage the good warfare, having faith and a good conscience, which some having rejected, concerning the faith have suffered shipwreck.

- Just as these instructions were given to Timothy by Paul, we are to remember the prophecies spoken over our lives, wage war with them, and fight well, knowing that the battle is the Lord's.
- Rely on God's Words and keep your faith and your conscience clear.
- However, some people have deliberately violated their consciousness, and they are shipwrecked.
- Aggressively use your prophetic Words as a weapon of warfare.
- Do not hold up and wait until the battle is over; take the Word of God and wage war.
- Do not put it on a shelf and wait for it to come to pass.
- Paul gave Timothy these instructions that it was not going to happen unless he did something.

What must we do with the prophesies spoken over our lives?

_____
_____
_____
_____

IGNITED AGAIN

DISCUSSION:

Timothy not only had prophetic words, but he also had Paul lay hands on him. Paul said to fan into flames those coals that are in you from the gift given by the Lord when I laid hands on you. The flame needs to be ignited by fanning the flame. You would think that if the Apostle Paul laid hands on you, he would have flames of fire coming out of his hands. But for some reason, it diminished to where they were just coals again in Timothy. Paul did not tell Timothy I will come and blow on those coals and make them into flames, or I will have to lay hands on you again. He said, you fan the coals into flames and be ignited again by taking those words and wage a good war in the Spirit over them.

❖ 2 TIMOTHY 1:6:

Therefore I remind you to stir up the gift of God which is in you through the laying on of my hands.

- The Words of prophecy will help you fight well in the Lord's battle.
- The Lord is in your midst, and the battle is His.
- The Lord will fight your battles because He has already labeled your enemies His enemies (Exodus 23:22).
- God has spoken, and He is going to keep His Words.
- When you say the Words and prophecies spoken, you are helping in the battle, and the battle is the Lord's because you have faith and trust in His words.

FREEDOM FROM FEAR

TRUTH IS A WEAPON

- ❖ **<u>2 CORINTHIANS 10:3-6:</u>**

For though we walk in the flesh, we do not war according to the flesh. For the weapons of our warfare *are* not carnal but mighty in God for pulling down strongholds, casting down arguments and every high thing that exalts itself against the knowledge of God, bringing every thought into captivity to the obedience of Christ and being ready to punish all disobedience when your obedience is fulfilled.

- Even though we are in the flesh and walk in this life, we are not waging war according to the flesh.
- The weapons of our warfare are not carnal. We have weapons, but they are not flesh and blood, but they are mighty in God for pulling down strongholds and casting down arguments.
- It does not say casting down evil spirits; it says, "casting down arguments and anything that exalts itself against the knowledge of God."
- God's Word, His revelation, and knowledge that was spoken are being contested by something.
- Evil spirits are promoting false ideas, and it is through witchcraft and evil people.
- The Lord says to label these things that exalt themselves and pull them down by defending the truth.

- ❖ If someone is saying something that is not correct, it needs to be corrected. If people think that it is God's Words and it is not, then it will not be in faith.

  - You won't get anything from something that God did not say.
  - You need to get rid of arguments and bring every thought into captivity to the obedience of Christ.
  - You need to get your doctrine right and the way you think right.
  - You can war and address the disobedience with the Word of God.

The weapons of our warfare are not carnal, but what are they?

_____
_____
_____
_____

STANDING IS A WEAPON

- ❖ <u>**EPHESIANS 6:10-13:**</u>

  Finally, my brethren, be strong in the Lord and in the power of His might. Put on the whole armor of God, that you may be able to stand against the wiles of the devil. For we do not wrestle against flesh and blood, but against principalities, against powers, against the rulers of the darkness of this age, against spiritual *hosts* of wickedness in the heavenly *places*. Therefore take up the whole armor of God, that you may be able to withstand in the evil day, and having done all, to stand.

- Paul is saying here that there are certain spiritual weapons, but most of them are defensive.
- One is aggressive and offensive, and that is the sword, whereas all the others are just defensive weapons.
- He says you stand and after you have done everything to stand firm, and this is because we have the truth.
- Truth is a weapon.
- Evil spirits will speak a lie, and you continually speak the truth.
- You have authority over evil spirits and address them and break their power.
- Evil spirits must listen to you.
- If Christians adhered to the truth, evil spirits would not be able to operate.
- People are deceived with false ideas and doctrines about themselves and God.
- Evil spirits have entered these people and embodied them.
- People have been hijacked.
- People manifesting evil spirits are in charge, in authority, with wicked agendas.
- Your battle strategies are to take up all the armor, be strong in the power of the Lord, and stand firm against the wiles or strategies of the wicked one.
- We wrestle against an antichrist spirit.
- We need to come against four different echelons or levels of these entities: the principalities, the powers, the rulers of the darkness of this age, and the spiritual host in Heavenly places.

- We take up the defensive weapons of the armor and the offensive one, which is the sword of the Spirit, the Word of God.
- A spiritual person is fortified with the truth.

DISCUSSION:

You must exercise all that has been established from the benefits of being a Christian, our righteousness, holiness, and all the understanding of God's will. The benefits of salvation that have been given us to keep our head in every situation and manifest Christ. Then through prayer and supplication in the Spirit, we are watchful to this end with perseverance and supplication for all the saints. So, we pray for all the saints. You pray for the body of Christ in the complete full armor of God, persevere, do not give in, and do not give up.

FORGIVENESS IS A WEAPON

❖ **2 CORINTHIANS 2:10:**

Now whom you forgive anything, I also *forgive*. For if indeed I have forgiven anything, I have forgiven that one for your sakes in the presence of Christ.

- Do not be ignorant of satan's devices by having you bound in unforgiveness.
- God is a warrior, and He has come into your environment to fight with you and for you on your behalf.

- God had all authority before we were ever in existence. He gives us His name, and we can use it.
- He is singing songs of deliverance over you.
- One of the enemy's battle strategies is to get you to be offended so you can be taken advantage of.
- Exercise your authority after you have forgiven.

LOVE IS A WEAPON

❖ I JOHN 4:18:

There is no fear in love; but perfect love casts out fear, because fear involves torment. But he who fears has not been made perfect in love.

- I know if I am not made perfect in love if I still have fear.
- You must deal with fear because you cannot have both fear and perfect love.
- If I am not established in perfect love, that fear will creep in, and fear involves torment.
- Remember, if Christ loved first and made us perfect in that love, we love Him because we know He made the initiative.
- He came to and loved us first, and God conquers fear through that love.

LOVE FOR GOD AND ONE ANOTHER

❖ 1 JOHN 4:1-3:

Beloved, do not believe every spirit, but test the spirits, whether they are of God; because many false prophets have gone out into the world. By this you know the Spirit of God: Every spirit that confesses that Jesus Christ has come in the flesh is of God, and every spirit that does not confess that Jesus Christ has come in the flesh is not of God. And this is the *spirit* of the Antichrist, which you have heard was coming and is now already in the world.

❖ 1 JOHN 4:4-6:

You are of God, little children, and have overcome them, because He who is in you is greater than he who is in the world. They are of the world. Therefore they speak as of the world, and the world hears them. We are of God. He who knows God hears us; he who is not of God does not hear us. By this we know the spirit of truth and the spirit of error.

- To be effective, we have instructions to test whether the spirits are of God.
- Every spirit that confesses Jesus Christ has come in the flesh is of God.
- The spirit of the antichrist will not confess that Jesus Christ is of God.
- You are of God's little children and have overcome them, so He who is in you is greater than he in the world.
- They are of the world; therefore, they speak as the world, and the world hears them.

- We are of God, and He who knows God hears us, and he who is not of God does not hear us.
- We will know the Spirit of Truth from the spirit of the air.

How can you tell if a spirit is of God or of the antichrist?

_____
_____
_____
_____

KNOWING GOD THROUGH LOVE

❖ **<u>I JOHN 4:7-11:</u>**

Beloved, let us love one another, for love is of God; and everyone who loves is born of God and knows God. He who does not love does not know God, for God is love. In this the love of God was manifested toward us, that God has sent His only begotten Son into the world, that we might live through Him. In this is love, not that we loved God, but that He loved us and sent His Son *to be* the propitiation for our sins. Beloved, if God so loved us, we also ought to love one another.

- Let us love one another, for love is of God, and everyone who loves is born of God and knows God.
- He who does not love does not know God, for God is love.

- God loved us and sent His only begotten Son of the world that we might believe and live through Him in this love and propitiation of our sins.
- If God so loved us, we ought to love one another.

SEEING GOD THROUGH LOVE

❖ **I JOHN 4:12-16:**

No one has seen God at any time. If we love one another, God abides in us, and His love has been perfected in us. By this we know that we abide in Him, and He in us, because He has given us of His Spirit. And we have seen and testify that the Father has sent the Son as Savior of the world. Whoever confesses that Jesus is the Son of God, God abides in him, and he in God. And we have known and believed the love that God has for us. God is love, and he who abides in love abides in God, and God in him.

- Actual warfare is when there is that transference of love.
- If we love God, God abides in us, perfecting His love in us.
- Warfare occurs when we label things, whether of God or an evil spirit.

TRANSFERENCE PRODUCES FRUIT

❖ **I JOHN 4:20-21:**

If someone says, "I love God," and hates his brother, he is a liar; for he who does not love his brother whom he has seen, how can he love God whom he has not seen? And this commandment we have from Him: that he who loves God *must* love his brother also.

- If someone says they love God and hate his brother, he is a liar.
- For warfare to be effective, it must be transferred from us individually.
- You receive the Word of God from this teaching, study, the Spirit of God speaks to you, and live out your daily life.
- The transference happens when it creates fruit—it produces fruit.
- What happens is it turns outwardly to where you are ministering outwardly.
- God is in your midst, and this is the transference.
- If God has loved you, then you love your brother, and the Spirit is here to manifest that.
- If God has delivered you, then you start to have the ability to speak deliverance and to minister.
- Deliverance to people can be healing, restoration of finances, and all kinds of things, including relationships.
- You are speaking the Good News of the Gospel.
- People are healed, delivered, saved, and people are being raised from the dead.
- These are all outward-aggressive signs of what has happened inside of you.
- God wants you to be delivered and free from fear.
- The result should be a war you win because you are aggressively administering this.

- **The disconnect in the body of Christ is receiving the Word of God, but there is no turning outward and ministering to each other and getting people saved. It needs to increase so that the power has to be there. The Lord has to be in your midst for you to be on fire.**

PRAYER

Father, I thank You for the perfect love You have given through Jesus Christ. Right now, we receive the spirit of love, power, and a sound mind. We receive that power right now, and we impart it to all of you right now. Father, I thank You so much that this drives out the fear, and it leaves everyone in the name of Jesus. We are being perfected in love, power, and authority in the name of Jesus.

SALVATION PRAYER

Lord God,
I confess that I am a sinner.
I confess that I need Your Son, Jesus.
Please forgive me in His name.
Lord Jesus, I believe You died for me and that You
are alive and listening to me now.
I now turn from my sins and welcome
You into my heart. Come and take control of my life.
Make me the kind of person You want me to be.
Now, fill me with Your Holy Spirit, who will show me how to live for You.
I acknowledge You before men as my Savior and my Lord.
In Jesus' name. Amen.

If you prayed this prayer, please contact us at
info@kevinzadai.com for more information and material.

We welcome you to join our network at Warriornotes.tv
for access to exclusive programming

To enroll in our ministry school, go to:
Warriornotesschool.com

Visit KevinZadai.com for additional ministry materials

About Dr. Kevin Zadai

Kevin Zadai, Th.D., was called to the ministry at the age of ten. He attended Central Bible College in Springfield, Missouri, where he received a Bachelor of Arts in theology. Later, he received training in missions at Rhema Bible College and a Th.D. at Primus University. Dr. Kevin L. Zadai is dedicated to training Christians to live and operate in two realms at once— the supernatural and the natural. At age 31, Kevin met Jesus, got a second chance at life, and received a revelation that he could not fail because it's all rigged in our favor! Kevin holds a commercial pilot license and is retired from Southwest Airlines after twenty-nine years as a flight attendant. Kevin is the founder and president of Warrior Notes School of Ministry. He and his lovely wife, Kathi, reside in New Orleans, Louisiana.

Other Books and Study Guides By Dr. Kevin Zadai

*Kevin has written over fifty books and study guides
Please see our website for a complete list of materials!
Kevinzadai.com*

60-Day Healing Devotional

60-Day Devotional: Encountering the Heavenly Sapphire

60-Day Devotional: The Holy Spirit

60-Day Devotional: Supernatural Finances

The Agenda of Angels

The Agenda of Angels: Study Guide

A Meeting Place with God, The Heavenly Encounters Series Volume 1

Days of Heaven on Earth

Days of Heaven on Earth: A Study Guide to the Days Ahead

Days of Heaven on Earth: Prayer and Confession Guide

Encountering God's Normal

*Encountering God's Normal: Study Guide
Encountering God's Will*

Encountering the Heavenly Sapphire: Study Guide

From Breakthrough to Overthrow: Study Guide

Have you Been to the Altar Lately?

Heavenly Visitation

Heavenly Visitation: Study Guide

Heavenly Visitation: Prayer and Confession Guide

*How to Minister to the Sick:
Study Guide*

It's Rigged in Your Favor

*It's all Rigged in Your Favor:
Study Guide*

*It's Time to Take
Back Our Country*

*Lord Help Me to Understand
Myself: Study Guide*

Mystery of the Power Words

*Mystery of the Power Words:
Study Guide*

*The Notes of a Warrior: The
Secrets of Spiritual Warfare
Volume 1: Study Guide*

*The Notes of a Warrior: The
Secrets of Spiritual Warfare
Volume 2: Study Guide*

*Operating In Kingdom
Authority: Study Guide*

*The Power of Creative
Worship: Study Guide*

*Prayer Nations
With Kevin & Kathi Zadai*

*Praying from the
Heavenly Realms*

*Praying from the Heavenly
Realms: Study Guide*

Precious Blood of Jesus

*Precious Blood of Jesus:
Study Guide*

Receiving from Heaven

*Receiving from Heaven:
Study Guide*

*Spiritual Discernment:
Study Guide*

*Stories from the Glory
with Sister Ruth Carneal*

Supernatural Finances

*Supernatural Finances:
Study Guide*

Supernatural Prayer Strategies of a Warrior: Study Guide

Taking a Stand Against the Enemy

Taking Off the Limitations

Taking Off the Limitations: Study Guide

The Vision and Battle Strategies of Warrior Notes Intl.

Unveiling the Mystery of the Prophetic: Study Guide

Warrior Fellowships Season 1 Volume 1: Study Guide

Warrior Fellowships Season 1 Volume 2: Study Guide

Warrior Notes Aviation Volume 1: Flight Manual Study Guide

Warrior Women Volume 1: Study Guide

Warrior Women Volume 2: Study Guide

Warrior Justice: A Study Guide to Experiencing Freedom from Demonic Oppression

You Can Hear God's Voice

You Can Hear God's Voice: Study Guide

Made in the USA
Columbia, SC
09 June 2023

17803377R00083